UNKNOWN CIVILIZATION OF PREHISTORIC INDIA

UNKNOWN CIVILIZATION OF PREHISTORIC INDIA

SUBHASHIS DAS

Kaveri Books
New Delhi-110002

Unknown Civilization of Prehistoric India with a complimentary chapter by Terence Meaden

Photograph by author.

Photo credits: Smt Bubu Das, Prantik (Bumpy) Das, Shib Shanker Goswami, Antony Roper Crerar, Terence Meaden, Nawaj Ud-Din and Author.

Illustration by Ujjwal Ghosh.

First Published in 2014
ISBN 978-81-7479-142-9

Published by
Kaveri Books
4832/24, Ansari Road
New Delhi - 110 002 (India)
Tel.: 011-2328 8140, 2324 5799,
Fax: 011-2328 8140
E-mail: kaveribooks@vsnl.com,
kaveribooks@gmail.com
Website: www.kaveribooks.com

Laser Typesetting by : Deep Graphics, Delhi

Printed at : Shree Balaji Art Press, Delhi - 110 053

PRINTED IN INDIA

This book is dedicated to all lovers of megaliths and
their unknown makers who were artists and
scholars par excellence and
who died unknown, unsung and unnoticed.

This book is also for
you Ma...

and even for you Kisku ji; some people are just unforgettable
even after when they have set out on that never returning journey...

PREFACE

Since the initiation of history writing in India historians both mainstream and alternative have sought the narratives of Indian history from diverse resources as archaeological data, their interpretation and along with assortment of literary texts. Linguistic evidences too have played quite a part in the construction of our country's prehistory.

Indian prehistory seems to be sitting pretty as long as tribal features do not impinge on it. Tribalism has not been brought into account while building India's prehistory nor its relics, the megaliths which have not been considered as venerated artefacts of Indian prehistory. Megalithism hides a complete different world within itself, entry into which may facilitate readers of Indian prehistory to look at it in a wholly new perspective. Tribal folklores deemed correctly by many as oral history not having received wide acceptance have been eschewed both by historians of the colonial era and of the post independence times. Nationalist writers have projected India's past with an interpretation of literary texts and archaeological relics born from their chauvinistic mindset which deprecates anything tribal.

The entire hoard of scholars correlate megaliths with death, which can be reckoned correct for a faction of these monuments but many of these primitive megaliths have a different story to tell. Modern research has revealed that precise geometry, horizon astronomy were used by the ancients in the assembling and building of many of these megaliths. That the primitive tribals were aware of such intricate sciences in hoary times is testified by these primitive megaliths which stand in stark contradiction to the established norm that astronomy and mathematics were the inventions of the Brahmanical scholars as Aryabhatta and Varahamihira.

The sudden surge of interest in megaliths amidst the younger populace has brought many of these primitive temples to light across the world revealing near similar to even stunningly identical architectures. What equally riveting is the alliance of near similar rituals, deities and ritualistic oblations regarding these megaliths. Scholars do not believe that connections between countries very far placed were feasible in the deep past owing to the inaccessible distances that kept them apart. But similar megalithic architecture, rituals and deities of the erstwhile fertility cult, along with similar methods for observation of the sun and other celestial bodies vide horizon astronomy through megaliths too lends credence to the fact that such a contact amongst each other in remote antiquity was a reality.

The tradition of proto austroloid Santals and Mundas speak of their traversing in a far off land where they had taken birth and their later ingress into India. Santali folktales speak of their one time journey into a colder region called Jarpi Desh which they now corroborate with Europe. Stumbling upon the numerous Mundari words in many European languages, names of many towns and villages and even many similar rituals which can only result from a contact between both peoples are possible evidences of such a migration in the deep past. The Mundari Kols also acknowledged as Hors; a term which they employ to designate themselves can be traced back to Genesis in the Old Testament.

Subsequent waves of proto austroloid Mundari tribals entered India through the North West frontiers of the country lugging with them their culture, religion and a brand of megalithism comprising astronomy and mathematics. That numerous names of villages, towns, rivers and hills in present day Afghanistan, Pakistan and India which has survived the tides of times are Mundari in origin confirm such a journey of these tribals into India through these tracks. It seems the megalithic Mundas had entered the country through Asota, Burzahom in Kashmir and an another wing of these Kols, perhaps the Santals and the Dravidian Kurukh speaking Oraons through the Harappan region.

A bulk of these adivasis has been clamouring since long that it had been them who were partially responsible for the Harappan civilization and their claim reverberates in their folktales and songs as testimonies. Santali legends affirm numerous tales and songs of their sojourn in the Indus region during their journey into India. For them the Indus River was *Sinjho Nai.* Bronze figures as that of the nude female from Mohenjo-Daro which seem possible. Dokra in its make confirm that this tribal art was prevalent in the Indus Valley. Jaidev Baghel, the eminent master Dokra craftsman art from Chhattisgarh, a Kolarian tribal himself too believes that Dokra was widespread in Harappa.

If all the above be true, which indubitably is, has not the time rightly arrived to confer a relook at our snugly put up prehistory and set things right under such new researches and finds ? Should we not scientifically test and retest the tribals' assertion cited in their folklores to help reconstruct a new past of ours? This book attempts to speak of this unspoken India, of this newly learnt dormant civilization which flourished around megaliths and in the process bring out that enigmatic phase of our country's prehistory not known to many.

I put into words my heartfelt gratitude to the eminent scholar, writer and archaeologist Terence Meaden of Oxford University who has kindly consented to pen his feelings in the book in a few pages that India and Britain do have much in common in many features of megalithic archaeology and which may have resulted from a contact in the antiquity.

I also thank my wife Bubu, son Prantik for their constant support and accompaniment in journey to the most inaccessible Maoist infested terrains in search of the primitive megaliths. My earnest thanks to Ms Lydia Ekeswalfe of Dresden Museum, Germany for encouraging me constantly and providing me with plentiful papers and journals for the research. Not to forget Antony Roper Crerar of Wales—my gratitude towards him for being an unvarying source of encouragement. My sincerest appreciations are for Shib Shanker Goswami, Aloke Rana, Abhisek Mishra, Amarnath Pathak and Sunil Agarwalla for their continuous encouragement and for believing in the kind of work I was doing. I also thank the brothers Arunangshu and Ajatshatru Chatterjee in helping me with the mathematics of the Jagannath Pahari and the megaliths of Punkree Burwadih. I need to tell to all of them that this book would not have seen the light of the day had it not been their cooperation and love backing me up. I can assure you this entire book will make an engrossing reading.

Subhashis Das

CONTENTS

List of Plates

FROM THE LOST CLOSET
OF
PRE-HISTORY

1 The Migrations

The eternal debate that who among the Aryans and Dravidians were indigenous to the land; is as old as the hills. A consensus doesn't seem to be in sight; each party comprising of archaeologists and historians put up testimonies which they regard as evidences to prove their point, further complicating matters. Amidst in this entire muddle, the tribal factor has been missed out as if they did not exist at all. Archaeologists and historians fighting it out on the issue are now indulged in allegations on one another of distorting the country's history. One faction hold the other responsible for what they call having too much western bias and/or are often branded as Marxist historians, who on the other hand charge the former as being politically enthused having fundamental Hindu favouritism opinions. Leaving aside such mudslinging which will lead them nowhere, they should dig deep into the history of the tribals for a change.

The tribals who though do not boast of any possible script, written literature, coins or any other archaeological artefacts possesses a very well preserved history of their community in the form of their folklores and tradition and in their archaeological relics known as megaliths.

Megaliths have always been ignored and shunned by archaeologists, historians, scholars and even by the common man. That these primitive stones could be artefacts of history appear to be a silly demand since megaliths being devoid of scripts or illustrations on them cannot be instrumental in reconstructing history. If only the tribal tradition, religion and rituals were known and recognized, much could have been correlated with the stones; their positioning, their shapes, sizes, architectures and their commonness with megaliths of all over the world. These speak an unspoken and unwritten language which can enable in rewriting our past.

The tribal traditions and legends are narrated and sung during their major ceremonies as births, marriage and child's naming and so on. Such folk traditions are rightly recognized today by many institutions in several countries as oral history. Folklores long enunciate interactions and contacts between cultures and civilizations in the remote past irrespective of enormous distances; a theory vehemently spurned by archaeologists and other scholars implying that such connexions simply could not have been achievable in the past. But similar names for people, towns and villages and even for the same objects among faraway lands are only few evidences among the plentiful which prove relationships between these lands in the ancient times.

How long such major sources of history should be chided as coincidences, instead of admitting them as evidences of relationships between civilizations in the ancient times? My former book **Sacred Stones in Indian Civilization** had elucidated with numerous testimonies that how migration was an ingredient of human existence and groups of people had constantly migrated from one part of the land to another since remote past till a few centuries ago. Folktales of the proto austroloid Kolarians do speak of such migration of having had rambling into various countries of the world in the past, including India.

It is difficult to assert that who were the original residents of India. Although proofs of both the Dravidians and the Aryans being outsiders are in abundance, many scholars have come forth to reject these theories and hold them native to the land. Many old scholars firmly believe that prior to their entry into India parts of the country were perhaps inhabited by the Mongoloid type people. I am also a firm supporter of this theory and believe that the Mongoloids had perhaps arrived from the South East of the country. The arrival of the proto austroloid Mundaric tribals and the Dravidians into the pristine land of India were perhaps prior to the entrance of the Aryans.

The migratory nature of our predecessors may had necessitated their movements from one land to the other. In such an exercise, food too may have been carried with them along with other essentialities. Niger and Millets of various variety of African origin was introduced into India in the 3rd-2nd Mill B.C. This is evidence of migrations occurring into India from Africa during such antiquity.[1] People had carried various trees and plants to where they had travelled. Trees like Baobab and Gulmohar was introduced into the country by the Muslim rulers[2]. Similarly, that Durra Sorghum is grown in the Muslim areas of both Africa and India confirms that it were the Arabs who must have carried them from India to Africa and Arabia.[3] Migration was not a single sided event as normally believed to be, but multi- directional. Why people moved, is an eternal enigma as no one perhaps can state for certain why people had once indulged in such activities. Many assign slash and burn agriculture for it, some recommend the cause to be the lack of hunt and water in their locale, while several suggest it was for the search of a better habitat and many would ascribe the migratory nature and the restless temperament of our ancestors which still haunts the modern vagabond.

Migration therefore has influenced the fate of many nations politically, socially and culturally. The introduction of various foods as mentioned above has remained instrumental in changing the food habits of nations much similar to the introduction of potato in India by the Moghuls that it is the most indispensable ingredient in Indian meals today. Archaeologists too are of the view that the stone axes in India were the result of the influences with migration from China.[4] Dani believed that the North East India was the meeting ground of various Axes and Adzes where the Indian tool had blended with the adze types from South East Asia[5] Gordon felt that the faceted chisels found in Lohardagga in Jharkhand were imports from Yunan, China.[6]

There are various testimonials which also confirm human movements even in the deep past. One such evidence are the street dogs which generally evade our attention of being solid proofs of human migrations having occurred somewhere in the past. Street dogs in particular are always an enigma to me. Wherefrom had these animals arrived and how did they spread all over the country or even across most of the parts of the world, are a few riddles which bewilders me. Why are these animals so prone to being tamed and how they can respond to love so spontaneously, is a mystery.

The find of so many dogs' graves all around disclose mankind's love and attachment towards these domesticated animals. Even next to my hometown there is a village called 'Seotagarha' which people have mutilated as 'Sitagraha' associating it with the mythical Sita. 'Seotagarha' has stemmed from the union of two austric words of 'Seota' meaning dog and 'garha' which is a burial. Seotagarha literally means a burial of a dog. Dogs have always remained the closest allies of the tribals. That these animals are everywhere suggests that ancestors of these dogs had accompanied their erstwhile tribal masters wherever they had wandered to. That the predecessors of these dogs had been living together with humans for a very long time is perhaps the answer for these animals' ability to love and be tamed. The tribals having long moved away left behind quite a number of their dogs whose descendants now rule the streets of every city and village in India. The ubiquitous dogs also confirm that India was a tribal country once prior to her Brahmanisation. Dogs have always been sneered in India by the Aryans as they have been regarded unholy and have coerced them away from sacred places.

Migration of the Aryans

B.B.Lal the former Director General of Archaeological Survey of India and one of the most revered archaeologists of the nation and his like-minded set of people firmly believe that Aryans were indigenous to this country. He has lately authored a book, **"How deep are the Roots of Indian Civilization, Archaeology Answers"** in which basing on a Vedic text he rightly mentions that an emigration of a band of Aryans did take place from India to Iran and Turkey in the ancient times around 1500 to 2100 BCE.

Before proceeding further may I but put forth a query to the honourable scholar; Is Indian civilization the civilization of the Aryans only? Why is it only the Aryan civilization should be synonymous to the Indian civilization? Don't the Dravidian and the tribal factors also play a part?

Indian civilization does not specifically stand for the Aryans, I spurn such concepts as India is a diverse land of numerous tribes, societies and religions therefore we need to embrace both the written and the oral histories of all religions and tribes into account for a valid history of our nation.

Reverting to our discussion on the migration of the Aryans, Lal puts forth a theory that the Aryans travelled to Central Asia from India. He translates the Bodhayan Srauthshastra (18.44) by narrating that the sons of Pururavas and Urvasi, Ayu and Anavasu migrated to the east and the west respectively[7]. No reason has been assigned by Bodhayana for this movement. Had settlement been the motive, then east was not a good tract as the place was not only densely forested but was also sparsely populated and 'barbaric' tribes and the 'sankirna jatis' of whom the Aryans were scared of hence despised, resided there. The region therefore was generally regarded as mlechhadesha.[8] Lal believes that the Aryans being indigenous to India one of their factions moved out of the country.

Lal rightly interprets the 'west' here as the region of Persia and Turkey to where Amavasu migrates. This region was densely populated during the period when Amavsau had travelled to Persia, it was here many kingdoms, and civilizations had risen and fallen. Why had Amavasu immigrated to such a place is unknown. Did he travel there to spread the Aryan Vedic religion?

We do not know for sure but chances are that an Aryan empire of the Mitannis may have been existing prior to the arrival of Amavasu here. His journey to this land therefore was predetermined. Amavasu may have travelled back to this land of the Aryans in Mitanni walking back on the track on which his predecessors had entered India.

Mitannis were believed to be in power at around 1600 BC. So the arrival time of Amavasu could have been possibly somewhere around this date. The Mittanis were originally an Indo European lot speaking the Indo Aryan Language but ruled the locals in the non-Indo Aryan Hurrian tongue; a fraction of these people may have had migrated to India[9]. Aggression always raged between the Mitannis and the Hittites and eventually an accord of amity was signed between the two warring factions. This is evident from the clay tablet found in an excavation in Boghazkoi in Turkey.

The relic was discovered to be a treaty between Mitanni and Hittite kings who surprisingly had Aryan names; and as for the witness to the treaty they invoked Vedic gods as Indra, Mitra and Nasdyas and Varuna. It is now known that the Mitannis had Aryan/Sanskrit names for themselves and they worshipped Vedic Gods.

This was also the land where even the Hurrians who may also have been called the Horites. The Horites were perhaps analogous with the ancestors of the proto austroloid Kolarian Hors as the Khadias, Mundas, Santals, Hos and other similar tribes of today who possibly were regarded as 'Asuras' in Indian Puranic and Vedic texts (we will deal this in a later chapter). Many also relate the Hittites to the Horites. D.B. Kisku also believed[10] that the both the tribals and the Aryans dwelled along with each other in Mitanni near the Caspian Sea.

Vedic texts do confirm that the Devas and the Asuras too initially had resided together in a region called 'Ilavritavarsha' which many regard as the 'Swarg rajya' which once translated in to plain English can be understood as the metaphoric heavenly abode.

At the beginning, the Devas and the Asuras; the Aryans and the tribals shared power and were also in good friendly ties with one another. The relationship which turned sour by the passing tides of time eventually resulted in a prolonged battle. The clashes are popularly known as the legendary; 'Devasura Yudha' or the battle between the Devas and the Asuras or the Aryans and the tribals. In this protracted battle both the parties won at some stage or the other. The Devas or the Aryans drove away the Asuras or the tribals from there as the war according to the Vedic texts was eventually won by the Aryan Devas. Are the Vedic texts referring to the conflict between the Mitannis and the Hittites? The proceedings look so similar, it could be. In the beginnings of the Rig Veda the Aryan Indra takes pride in calling himself an Asura. Later however when their relationships turns sour the same Indra becomes the largest slayer of the Asuras killing hundreds of non-Aryan (anarya) tribals and destroying similar number of their purs or their cities.

Even tribals are known to retain many Vedic names as Varun and Sambar, for themselves and many even keep the lesser known Rig Vedic gods as Bandhu and Pusa as their names. Such a norm of having Aryan names could unknowingly go back to the good old friendly days when both the 'Devas' or the Aryans and the 'Asuras' or the tribals lived happily together in Central Asia. The Santal tradition also talk of an ancestral land called *Aere Disom* during their meandering in this region which once converted in to simple English could mean "The Country of the Aryans". If the Santali interpretation is proper then chances are that Aere Disom was perhaps the land of the Mitanni Empire.

References

1. M.D. Kajale. Antiquity of Native African Millets and Associated Plants with some Observations on Prehistoric Plant Introductions into the Indian Subcontinent. Introduction of African Crops into South Asia. Indian Society for Prehistoric and Quaternary Studies.
2. H.Santapau. Common Trees. NBT
3. K.L.Mehra. Dispersal of plant cultivators between Prehistoric Africa and South Asia. Introduction of African Crops into South Asia. Indian Society for Prehistoric and Quaternary Studies.
4. D.H.Gordon. The Prehistoric background of Indian culture. Munshiram Manoharlal Publishers Pvt. Ltd.
5. A.H.Dani. The Prehistory and proto-history of Eastern India. The prehistory and proto history of Eastern India. Thesis in Indian Archaeology for London University.
6. D.H.Gordon. The Prehistoric background of Indian culture. Munshiram Manoharlal Publishers Pvt. Ltd.
7. B.B.Lal. How deep is the Indian Civilization? Archaeology answers. Aryan, New Delhi.
8. Romila Thapar. The Past and the Prejudice. National Book Trust. New Delhi.
9. www.historyfiles.co.uk
10. D.B.Kisku. The Santals and their Country, Career Press.

2 THE MILIEU

Were the black skinned megalithic Mundas responsible for the construction of Stonehenge and other megaliths?

Sounds preposterous? But how do you explain the facts that both the megalithic Mundas in Jharkhand state of East India and the ancient Britishers call megaliths with the same term; Sasan and also the legend prevalent in the Callanish megaliths that black men arrived there in boats to build the megalith under the direction of a white priest[1]. That there was a contact between India and Britain was also understood by scholars of the colonial era like Keshab Chandra Sen. So when the British came to rule over India, Sen was quick to identify India with them as, "...we see a reunion of parted cousins, the descendents of two different families of the ancient Aryan race..." he however deemed the connection between the two countries in the ancient times in the Aryan perspective[2].

Megaliths are certainly one of the largest mysteries to haunt the present day humankind. Perhaps we shall never know why the first megaliths were ever made. No one can give a straight answer to that, but we can speculate from the relationship of the tribals with their sacred stones and megaliths which they or their ancestors had erected or they still erect.

The other question which comes to mind is why and how megalithism spread across the world. Did it have a cradle from where it all started or did it have a common uprising across the world? Straightforward answers cannot be expected for such questions also. Looking at the much similar megalithic structures all over the world, along with identical names for the same rituals, ritualistic objects, towns, rivers, hills and deities among countries very far placed, it can be surmised that not so many things can have a universal rising at the same time across the world. Communities in their course of their wandering may have carried their rites and beliefs along with the megalithic tradition along with them to the newer lands.

Tribes such as Santhals, Mundas, Hos, Sabaras, Asurs and the Dravidian speaking Kurukh believe that they were born outside India. Their traditions speak of their migration all over the world and in the process; one wing is believed to have entered India. These tribes anthropologically belong to the proto austroloid group and most of them are known to speak various forms of the Mundari language which is austric in origin. These speeches were once spoken from Afghanistan to the Mekong valley by a majority of the denizens of the land. These austric tribals largely raise megaliths after their death. The Santhals however do not have a megalithic tradition but whether they had it the past, is difficult to articulate.

According to the Santhal folklore they had spread all over the world and in the process they had even entered a cold region called Jarpi Desh, this they identify with Europe. There is however an uncanny resemblance between the names 'Europe' and the so called 'Jarpi' of the Santals. The presence of many austric Mundari words in Flemish, German, and Latin and in a few more European languages does confirm that such a migration of these Kolarian tribals may have had occurred sometime in deep antiquity.

The world is full of resemblances and researches are on to document them and even search for the probable basis for such similarities. One such a mysterious contact which is now gaining grounds is between primitive India and South America.

Talking of the Mayas, the name itself conjures many a mysteries; as it is similar to the Mayas described in the Ramayana and the Mahabharata. Maya in Indian scriptures was the name of an extremely accomplished architect who was capable of constructing extraordinary buildings. Although the name Maya is followed with a surname Danava meaning a giant could designate towards the enormous strength that was perhaps required to raise such colossal structures.

One web presentation speaks of one Dr. V.Ganapati Sthapati whose ancestors are believed to have constructed the eminent temple of Tanjore in the past had travelled to Peru to study the pyramids of the Mayans. He was more than surprised to find the Maya pyramids and a temple in the Incan Machu Pichu to possess the same measurements and 'geometric matrix' mentioned in Maya Danava's ancient book on architecture called "Vasati".

Dr. Sthatapati also discovered that the cubit used in the construction of the pyramids was akin to the primitive standard yard of ancient India known as the 'Kisku yard' which is approximately 33 inches.

The Kisku yard was also the cubit in building the houses in Harappan cities hence it was also known as the 'Indus gaz'[3] which is also very close to the megalithic yard initiated by Alexander Thom. (*What is particularly odd here is the term 'Kisku', which is not a Sanskrit but an austric term, rather Santhali; the language which had spread across a great section of the world in the ancient period along with them. 'Kisku' is very popular as a surname among the Santhals which is also their totem or 'kili'. Kisku also means a king among the austric Mundari speaking Santhalis.*)

The basic similarity between the Mayans and the Asuras/Rakchasas is their aboriginal origin. That the ancient Indian texts describe the Rakchasas as being blood thirsty places them next to the Mayans whose rituals having revealed a preponderance of blood and gore is also another parallel between both these communities. Mayas are found to have been featured in the Ramayana and subsequently in the Mahabharata and even in the Tamil Silappathikaram. According to the Mahabharata, Maya Danava was a stunning architect of buildings and his fame as a builder it seems transcended boundaries. The magnificent palace of the Pandava's in Indrapastha revealed Maya Danava's stunning skill as a virtuoso architect.

As exemplified in the ancient epics, it seems Maya is a race of people endowed with a grand expertise in architecture rather than an individual gifted with deftness in civil engineering. The palaces and the pyramids of the Mayas too were much splendid and the kind of astronomy which was involved in their construction showed these tribals' deep understanding of these sciences. There is a controversy regarding the author of Surya Siddhanta, a major work on astronomy and mathematics in early India. Many believe the text to have written by Maya Danava himself. These affinities between the mythical Maya of Indian epics and the Maya of South America do indicate towards the fact that both these set of people could be same.

Another similitude between South America and India lies in Tiuanaco in distant Bolivia where 'Birakocha' is hailed as a God who was believed to have sailed in from the east and is seen to be portrayed on a menhir. This is startling as because menhirs too in many parts of India are called 'Birakhoda' and 'Birakhola' which sound quite similar to Birakocha[4].

Scholars believe that in remote antiquity the world was matriarchal and practised the fertility cult. Prior to the Aryanisation of India and the advent of Brahminical deities, India like rest of the primitive world was carpeted by this archaic fecundity cult. Under such a faith the land, the rivers, hills and mountains and even the trees were revered as Goddesses. Traces of this once strong religion can still be found in many forms across India merged with the sankritised Hinduism. In the North East of India where Brahminisation has not been successful in putting much of its sway on the primitive religion of the tribals, the primitive fecundity cult persists. Society is still matrilineal and megaliths are still raised in the glory of the omnipresent Mother Goddesses. Sadly, the tribals' conversion to Christianity is hampering pagan megalithism here.

That India had a non-Aryan tribal past much before she was Aryanised, can be testified by the presence of so many primitive megaliths all over the land which are the archaeological remains of the once strong tribal dominance over India in the past. Unfortunately, not many people are aware of this phenomenon, as they do not pay much heed to either tribalism or megaliths. The archaic megaliths are everywhere from Kashmir to Kerala and from Tripura to Gujarat still they have been ignored by the scholars and archaeologists as insignificant relics of our prehistory.

Archaeologists have given the least importance to the surface architecture of these monuments hence much has been missed out. If they would have studied the surface architecture of the megalithic complexes with the same graveness they did to the burials below them, then we could have re- written our prehistory.

The surface positioning of many prehistoric megalithic complexes reveal that these monuments have been created to mathematical principles. Such megaliths also give evidence that the primitive megalithic folks were certainly not uncivilized barbarians as normally believed to be but apart from being knowledgeable in mathematics, they also had profound knowledge in observational astronomy. These unknown tribal megalithic mathematicians and astronomers were aware of these sciences thousands of years prior to Brahmin mathematician- astronomers as Bodhayana, Aryabhatta and Varahamihira *et al.*

But it was not only in India where the megalithic folks were well conversant in mathematics and astronomy but wherever in the world they raised the primitive megaliths, they did it to mathematical tenets and astronomical observations. The shapes of the menhirs convey an unwritten universal language, as many of their shapes across the world are similar[5].

Megaliths all over the world were not just burials, they were also temples and observatories and calendars. Therefore the synthesis of religion and science may have originated much before in the hoary antiquity whose blooming we observe in ensuing periods having evolved in the form of megaliths.

References

1. Julian Cope. The Modern Antiquarian, Thorsons.
2. Romila Thapar. The Past and the Prejudice, NBT.
3. Chris Knight & Robert Lomas. Uriel's machine, Fairwinds Press.
4. Subhashis Das. Sacred Stones in Indian Civilization, Kaveri Books.
5. Ibid.

3 A Past Which is Still Unknown

India's prehistory is unknown to many; there are a lot of many questions in it which have still remained unanswered. We accept theories provided by the scholars whom they feel are correct hence we too think it to be the final truth.

The common man never questions–they are satisfied what they have been taught as they have many other things to mind; rising prices, career of their daughters and their sons...... what not...but if they would have known of the abundant similarities among civilizations placed far off would many not have questioned, how such a phenomenon did occur?

Question needs to be put forth, firstly to ourselves and then to the objects right away and finally to the experts who are sure to deny any remotest chance of a possible contact which may have had occurred among countries in the past.

If you ask them how is it megaliths, are known with the same name of sarsen or sasan in both UK and Jharkhand? Why the symbols that are found inside the megalithic chamber of Garvinis in UK can also are seen made on the homes of many sedentary communities in India? Plenty of icons seen in the rock art cave of Chauvet, France can also be found in the rock arts of Isko in Hazaribag, India. Why? Why are so many megalithic architectures common all over the world? Why names of many towns, villages, hills, rivers and so on in far off countries are same irrespective of the distances that keep them apart? Even names for the same object can be found to be similar among countries placed diametrically opposite to each other, why?

There are more, many more questions but for each of them the scholars would shrug and quip with a smile, "Well, you see, all these are kind of strange for which there are no explanations...." or even, "You see all these seem very interesting, but... ... hmm, let's see... ah well... the world is full of coincidences..."

Why be so complex when the answer is simple, very simple; the similarity could come only as a result of a contact between cultures in remote antiquity and nothing else.

I will try to locate many such similarities between India and other countries and cultures which I believe must have emerged due to a communication with each other in the past. Tracing this primitive contact is a difficult task, indeed. But I believe that the folklores of the Kolarian tribes have much to offer, if only we have faith in their tradition, a new prehistory of India may dawn.

Perhaps the tribals and their archaeology of megaliths have not been taken into serious consideration by the scholars therefore they remain shunned from the domains of the prehistory of India. Meaningful research has still not been attempted on the folklores of the tribals and their megaliths. Whenever we speak of our own prehistory, we put forth the Indus valley Civilization and in the process, the rest of the country draws a complete blank. For the common man, India in her deep antiquity was either a monotonous land of wandering band of primitive cannibalistic savage tribes with stone tools to hunt animals in the dense woods or eat other humans or perhaps the country for them was comprised of implausible mythical characters not endorsed by archaeology.

Yes, tribes did lead a nomadic life and they did live in transitory shacks. We must always understand that living in make shift nomadic homes, practising slash and burn farming and utilising stone tools and eating on leaf plates does not necessarily make the primitives less civilized as normally believed to be. If Krishna and his set of Yadavas are not regarded as barbarians although they were nomads[1] then it is also incorrect to deem all the prehistoric nomadic tribals as savages. This notion that the primitives were less civilized has possibly stemmed in our minds from childhood schooling; it lies engraved today in our subconscious, something which is hard to do away with.

Many scholars have now begun to accept the various evidences which the amateurs had perceived many years earlier. That an unknown civilization thrived in many parts of the world in the remote past has been hypothesised by many. Acceptance has gradually crept in that there were constant communications between pre-Columbian America and the rest of the world or that America was inhabited by many tribes centuries prior to Columbus *et al.* Connexions between UK and India, South America and India have already been discussed in my former book and there are numerous other evidences which still lie interspersed all over the globe which authenticate communications between cultures in the past.

Even their languages can be found having similar words for the same object which were perhaps loaned from one another. It can also be seen that far placed lands share numerous affinities in art, culture, rituals, music, dances, food habits and many more things. If all these are not proofs of communication between civilizations and cultures at some very hazy antiquity in prehistory, then what is?

The commonness of culture is indeed the consequence of human contact between civilizations in the distant past or perhaps many as Graham Hancock and likeminded people speak of a common origin of our present civilization. The search and study of such an unknown history of humankind is both a tedious and an interesting exercise.

The veneration of Goddess Ur originating in Sumeria /Chaldea spread all over Europe and even ancient England. Her glory was profoundly influensive and it was brought even to India. She was the primeval Goddess of fertility and her presence in many names of towns and villages in India as Urimari, Urma, and Urband, Kanimurwar etc as suffix or prefix or even in its middle shows the kind of influence she had over the denizens of the villages at a very ancient period. The hibiscus flower is still known as Urhul which is a word formed from the terms Ur and hul, in plain English this would mean the 'hul' or flower for 'Ur'. The flower therefore was perhaps used in the worship of Goddess Ur[2]. The other Goddess was Ver or War who too was a fertility Goddess placed only subsequent to Ur[3].

Today these Goddesses have vanished with the passing time and the gradual Aryanisation of the land, but Ur and Ver/War still lives after the both have been combined to become Urwar or Urber which means fertility in Hindi.

Who were these people?

The ancient megaliths are a product of a civilization we know so very little of. Their sciences, their arts and their religion were much different from what we have known so far. My last book, *The Sacred Stones in Indian Civilization* showed how during an unknown period the stone models of the Jagannath Pahari were cut and shaped by an anonymous set of primitives to utilize them to study mathematics. These models neither house any script nor any artwork but they have been cut in accordance to precise mathematical measurements and shapes.

"Surya Sidhanta" is an ancient text of mathematics and astronomy in India which elucidates that the madhyarekha which is the indigenous prime meridian of Indian astronomy emerges from the South Pole and passes precisely through Lanka and the old cities of Avanti (modern Ujjain) and Rohitaka (modern Rohtak) on it way to

'Sumeru' or the North Pole. Either such an alignment could be an occurrence of coincidence or the place which may have later flourished into cities had been purposefully positioned by these people of this unknown civilization to let the madhyarekha pass through them, years prior the ancient book was written.

A query naturally emerges in mind whether all the primitive megaliths primarily the ones having proclivity towards astronomy were created by the tribals? The enquiry is obvious, as today the tribals do not disclose such knowledge in mathematics nor in astronomy, where has all their wisdom gone? The modern tribal megaliths may bear a resemblance to the ones of their ancestor's but both could be dissimilar serving separate purposes. If the contemporary megaliths are simply sepulchral or burial then the ancient ones apart from being so also discharged the duty of a boundary post, memorial for various social activities and even as astronomical stones.

If only the primitive megaliths, their measurements, inclines, places of their positioning, their orientations and alignments towards other megaliths (irrespective of distances), hills, cardinal points, major sun, moon and star rises would have been properly investigated then by now we would have had rewritten our country's prehistory and that of our world two times over. Can it be that such megaliths having implications towards the primitive sciences of astronomy and mathematics were created by a different race of people erudite in these sciences and the megalithic tribal merely built them according to their guidance?

An interesting proposition of which there are no evidences but then asking such a question is obvious. If the tribals did create these megaliths of Punkree Burwadih, Jagannath Pahri, Rola, Hanamsagar, Nilurallu then where has the knowledge among the tribals gone today? They do not even have a script therefore can such megaliths with mathematics be created without knowing any form of writing? We shall however discuss this enigma in some late chapter.

What we know of our prehistory is much different; megaliths have the capacity to change much of it. It requires courage to accept it, more so to write about it. The ancients accomplished incredible feats with their megaliths and even with their various unnamed sculptures of stones; all have gone unnoticed hence are not known to many which requires to be told to all.

References

1. Vishnu Purana, Gupta Press.
2. Subhashis Das. Sacred Stones in Indian Civilization. Kaveri Books.
3. Julian Cope. The Modern Antiquarian, Thorsons.

4 THE FERTILITY CULT

Scholars propose that the prevailing ancient world was matriarchal and matrilineal hence the matriarchs and the females were held in the highest esteem. The ancient earth was a female principle who dominated their lifestyle. Their Gods too were female and the religions they pursued were based on the archaic fertility cult of the primeval Mother Goddess. The fertility cult of the Great Mother swept the entire expanse of the primitive world; the earth itself was her representation. They walked on her, lived and died on her and to celebrate her glory raised fascinating stones temples of varied architectures on her which we know today as megaliths.

The primary motive behind their pursuing of the fertility cult was perhaps growth and multiplication of their families and tribes. Produce of lands as now must have become a key characteristic of this primitive religion. In India, lands are still valued by its fertility and so are woman. In rural societies, infertile women are still looked with disdain.

The colour red or ochre was possibly acquired from the colour of the menstrual blood. The similar coloured sindoor or vermilion applied by the married women on the partion of their hair and on their forehead was therefore a metaphor declaring their fertility and their ability to conceive[1]. Widows therefore abstain from putting on the feritly symbol of the vermillion, as she cannot conceive, in absence of her husband. The Grihasutras, on domestic ceremonies strongly instructs Aryan females to refrain from donning this anarya / non-Aryan practice of applying vemillion/sindoor[2]. Sindoor was detested by the Aryans, as it was an ingredient of the fertility cult of the earlier tribals of India which the patriarchal Aryans wanted to put a check on to.

Pregnancy must have been held in the highest esteem and pregnant woman revered. Watching a women's belly enlarge during pregnancy must have immensely amused the ancients and it was sacred as it contained the unborn and once born, a new leaf was to be added to the family creeper tree. Therefore, pregnant women were revered so much so that precise shapes of hills having bulges were considered the pregnant womb of women which became the emblem of the pregnant Recumbent Mother Goddess all over the world. Childbirth also fascinated them hence the female vulva through which the child was born and the womb where the unborn resided became revered entities. Circles, cracks, holes, and crevices on trees, on the soil, and everywhere were eyed as the vulva of the Goddess. These natural formations became the goddesses' symbols, hence are still venerated like in the olden times. Apart from the vaginal representations, rounded hills were also considered the Mother's breasts.

Death was not looked separately from life as it projected the act of returning to her womb as many deceased have been found placed inside stone circles in the foetal position. Many scholars believe that such positioning was due to their longing for a return to the mother's womb from where they had emerged. And when agriculture arrived, it was perhaps the first time when the primitives disassociated themselves from the string which tied them to the Great Mother[3] but she became mandatory for their newly found exercise; fertility became the prime characteristic of this cult. Observational astronomy became indispensable to this cult as the sun and moon rises on significant days determined the augmentation and the plummeting of productiveness of the land.

Fertility paintings on rock walls now changed surfaces and were visible on the walls of the village huts across the world which are still adorned with various illustrations symbolising the omnipresent Mother Goddesses of the archaic fertility cult. The vulva, the phalluses; auxiliaries of this cult can be found on utensils and other objects of day to day usage[4]. How did the glory of this archaic Goddess spread all over world is not known with certainty but perhaps it were the consequetive surge of primitive migrators who carried her splendour along with them wherever they went[5].

According to the opinion of the scholars, the primitive humanity was ignorant of the male's role in impregnation. Forces of nature, they believed were responsible for inseminating the females. For them it was the wind, the fire, the sun, a dip in a holy river or even the conducting of rituals on specific days in megalithic sites or even in caves which they believed was catalytical in the conception of the females[6]. The sun was also considered as the inseminator in the earlier days[7].

The Baigas also believed that the sun impregnated women on specific days and also that conception in a woman also happened if she bathed closed to her periods.[8] These, they regarded to be the appliances of fertility, therefore were highly revered. It was after the onset of animal husbandry males became conscious of their role in the impregnation of their womenfolk[9].

Times changed but these antiquated beliefs can still be seen in rural India where forces of nature are still unconsciously given importance for impregnation of the women. Infertile women still prefer to go through various impregnation rites mentioned above.

It is still a taboo for the belles to go open haired outside the house after dark; the prime reason being a certain tree in the neighbourhood which could be the home of a 'deota' (a god) or a 'daitya' (a giant) who may impregnate them.

Evidences of such primitive mode of impregnation by the forces of nature are in plenty in the ancient Brahmanical texts. Rig Veda states that impregnation is possible from the semen of the Agni or fire.[10] Even the Ramayana and Mahabharata mention such births because of the influence of the various forces of nature which were deified in ancient India. The birth of Hanumana is one such an instance which is cited in the Ramayana. Despite his biological father Kesari, Hanumana is said to have been born to the wind, which personified, as a god called Pawan Dev was believed to have impregnated his mother Anjana. Sugriva's mother was the wife of king Riksha, yet she too is believed to be made pregnant by the sun. In Mahabharata the birth of the four sons of Kunti; Karna, Yudhisthira, Arjuna and Bhima owes to the "blessing" of the sun, rain (Indra), wind, and fire all deified in India as gods.

That such stories of impregnation by forces of nature are abound in ancient Indian texts are confirmation of the documentation of such archaic thought and belief brought down from an even earlier source when times were matriarchal and the primitive populace was unaware of the male's role in conception.

Different Hindu communities have diverse rituals in regards to impregnation identified as 'god varai' or the 'filling up' of the womb. The name 'Godavari' for a major river in Central India perhaps indicates to such primitive beliefs that bathing in this sacred mother river could have resulted in an infertile woman's impregnation, a tradition perhaps coming down from hoary matriarchal days The river's impregnating attributes was perhaps one of the many causes had the ancestors hold the river holy.

The ancients' unexpected and sudden knowledge of the male's role in the impregnation of women coincided with the invention of iron; a metal harder than all the previous copper and bronze implements. Its firmness became synonymous with the male erection; the sword thereafter became the ultimate icon of manhood[11]. Iron therefore became symbolic of the phallic male whereas stone was submissive, soft yet tough, hence was female. The discovery of iron and the sudden acquirement of the male's knowledge of their role in the conceiving of the female changed the world completely, forever that much of the past could not even be recognized ; the rise of individuality followed soon after. Julian Cope cites Anne Bancroft's book, "Origin of the Sacred", "... with the abandonment of stone for the increasing use of metal. Something changed in people's hearts".[12]

How true was Bancraft that something did transform in their hearts and the advent of metals like iron in particular had the male confidence soar, shunning off their nanny jobs now it was their turn to call the shots. The forthcoming times witnessed an upsurge of violence along with the advent of an era where the males yearning for power and supremacy had them invent many warring weapons. There are plenty evidences scattered all over the country which confirms that the world had witnessed an era of unrelenting bloodshed, something never perceived before. This phenomenon's occurrence was perhaps due to the transformation of the world from the erstwhile female supremacy to the later evolved patriarchy.

The quality and the intensity of battles multiplied many a fold; killing never had been so easy[13]. Numerous evidences across the world including that in India show how Iron Age folks of the later ages had demolished the erstwhile habitation sites of the Neolithic people and even the megaliths of the former Mother Goddess people[14]. The patriarchal and violent Iron Age people put up phalluses on the female megaliths[15] proclaiming the male dominancy over the female shrine. To register their authority they had raised many a phalluses on many megaliths in Europe.

The primitive Rola megalithic site of Hazaribag has a small yet a splendid phallus, whether this too was erected for the same purpose we have no idea, but the site does not exhibit any sign of violence.

With the emergence of the male supremacy and the invention of iron across the world, a new religion began to evolve superseding the former Mother Goddess cult. In India, the fertility religion continued but it amalgamated with the newly born religion of the male oriented Gods of the Aryans. Many tribal and Dravidian Goddesses were Aryanised, many even had their names changed, and many deities were even disowned. These new people who trailed the Dravidians and the Kolarian Hors in to India brought in a male oriented and dominated religion in stark contrast to the female oriented and dominated docile fertility religion of the Great Mother with a mother child-proclivity. No wonder during the patriarchal Vedic ages we find the condition of women to having slipped to the lowest rungs of the social ladder.

References

1. Julian Cope. The Modern Antiquarian. Thorsons.
2. Subhashis Das. Sacred Stones in Indian Civilization. Kaveri Books.
3. Julian Cope. The Modern Antiquarian. Thorsons.
4. Ibid
5. Terence Meaden. The Secrets of Avebury Stones. Souvenir Press.
6. Verrier Elwin. The Baiga, Gyan Books.
7. Subhashis Das. Sacred Stones in Indian Civilization. Kaveri Books
8. Rig Veda. Sukta 68 7-8, Maruti Prakashan.
9. Subhashis Das. Sacred Stones in Indian Civilization. Kaveri Books.
10. Julian Cope. The Modern Antiquarian. Thorsons
11. Subhashis Das. Sacred Stones in Indian Civilization. Kaveri Books.
12. H.D.Sankalia. Prehistory of India, Munshiram Manoharlal Publications.
13. Julian Cope. The Modern Antiquarian. Thorsons.

5 THE ACCESSORIES OF THE FERTILITY CULT

Non-technological primitive societies under the matriarchal structure held women in the highest esteem. Wombs, enlarged bulges of hills; representative of pregnant bellies, cracks, crevices, circles; all symbols of the female genitals became deities of worship as all these represented the Great Mother Goddess. The numerous stone yonis of the Silwar Hill valley, the vulva of the black massif of the Jabra road Recumbent Mother Goddess, the stone yonis of Birbir and Honhe are all testimonials of this primitive worship. The megaliths were a product of this primordial Mother Goddesses' worship. The cult of the Mother Goddess is still prevalent among the non-Christian matrilineal Khasis of Meghalaya who consider the primeval omnipotent Mother Goddess as "Ka Yobai"[1].

This religion was therefore concomitant with fertility; the capability and potentiality to produce and grow must have been held in high esteem and there must have been customs pertaining to this. Even to this day most rituals, customs, and worship among village women are absorbed in primitive fertility practices.

Among the many fertility festivals still practised in India, "Jeetiya" is one which soon comes to mind. The mother observes the ceremony on the eighth lunar day of the month of 'Bhadra' during the monsoon. She prays to the fertility Goddesses and seeks her blessings for the well being of her children and also so that her family tree grows in all directions. Therefore climber vegetables such as '*satpathia*', '*jhinga*' and '*noni sag*' (a type of spinach) etc which spread rapidly in multi directions are representative of a long string of their family are put as offerings to this Goddess. Worshipping mothers therefore implore to the Goddesses for augmentation of their families in the manner of the creepers. These ancients rites lay much emphasis to the '*badhath*' or 'growth' of their family and their community hence these conventions are in contrary to the government's various population controlling measures, as the Hindus and the tribals still worship for expansion of their families and communities; no wonder India's population has been swelling leaps and bounds.

Copulation became a thing of worship which continues to be so in primitive cultures like that of India. Cultivating the female earth with the phallic plough was perhaps the supreme most union of both the sexes as similar to human unification of both the genders the former too resulted in production. The arrangement of the tall obelisk of Birbir and the phallus of Rola is done in such a manner that from a distance they are made to "fit on" the "V" cleft of the Great Recumbent Mother Goddess form of the Zulzul pahari signifying the female vulva ; the effect of the positioning is therefore the demonstration of the sacred intercourse.

Vegetables, it can be assumed have been executing the task of the principal component of many worship in India without which loads of rituals could not have been accomplished. The type of vegetables that are offered to the deities indicate to a tradition coming down from the much ancient period of the then prevailing fertility cult.

Vegetables as carrots, radishes and sweet potatoes etc which grow beneath the earth and are phallic in shape are male representations. Their growth inside the soil apparently implies to the sexual union with the earth which is a female principle. The other vegetables which are offered as '*chadhawas*' or offerings are yield of creepers as beans, '*Jhinga*', '*satpathia*', and so on. Owing to their characteristics of branching out creepers and their produce are therefore deemed as correct representatives of the budding and expanding family tree.

Cucumber[2], brinjal and banana etc are few other phallic fruits and vegetables which also are offerings in many fertility festivals. Vegetables too have their female counterparts as the fig[3], pumpkin and mango etc which are gifts to the Goddesses due to their fecundity characteristics and even due to their close akiness to the female womb. '*Teej*', '*Jeetia*' etc are some among the many fecundity ceremonies which are still conducted primarily by the women folk at homes which have not been Sanskritised, yet; meaning male Brahmin priests and the Sanskrit mantras are therefore not mandatory in these rites (till date).

That rites in such ceremonies are performed specifically by married females and mothers therefore is demonstration of the fact that the ancient fertility rituals have unabatedly been passed down the ages while being least influenced by Brahmanical beliefs and religion.

That much of Brahmanical forms of worshipping have evolved from a more primitive source is evident from the presence of many archaic fertility customs in them. In Hindu worship the kalash or the water pitcher is actually the fertility pot denoting the sacred womb and its nine-day worship is symbolical of the nine-month dwelling of the baby in the mother's womb[4]. A pitcher may also represent the egg which also signifies fertility[5]. Water sprinkled by the priest on the devotees from such pots is considered as '*subh*' or is believed to bring good luck and peace. In actuality water of such pitchers were once believed to possess oracular qualities bringing fertility[6].

The preliminary mantras uttered in every Hindu puja, is a plea to the Goddess to bless them so that their food reserve remains stacked up with grains. Such worship is affirmation that the origin of this tradition of worshipping lies deep in the Neolithic times during the inception of agriculture and the learning of the science of stocking the produce in stack baskets or *golas* (which too is incidentally was a female discovery).

Wells are also the symbol of the womb of the Great Goddess and water from it is consecrated as it encourages fecundity therefore is a necessity for the bride to conduct a particular ritual during marriages. The *Kusha* or the copper utensil in which the sacred water is stored resembles a fish which too is an icon of fertility. Water placed in it is therefore oracular and it sprinkled by the priest is certainly sacred, worthy of bringing productiveness.

Fish, primarily the Rohita or Rehu (*Labeo rohita*)[7] has been held in the highest esteem since Harappan days perhaps for the countless eggs it lays and the vaginal form it reveals once sliced. The Rehu fish is one of the most essential ingredients in marriage rituals among Bengalis.

In Bengal, I have also seen tiny vaginal shaped sweetmeats called 'gujia' which are offerings to deities. (Pl.49) 'Gujia' in simple Bengali would mean an object within which something could be inserted, which obviously implies to the female genitals. During Diwali among the North Indian states small female statues carrying fish, water pot or even holding the 'diya' or the earthen lamp (Pl.2) are worshipped by the rural women particularly by the unmarried belles which are instruments of the fertility cult still practised by the rural women folk. Such evidence of the erstwhile fertility cult of the Mother religions still lie widely scattered across the sacred land of India, many of which has been left unaltered by the patriarchal Vedic religion.

The elephant and the turtle were aboriginal in origins which too were worshipped as fertility motifs. They were however acculturated into Buddhist and Hindu symbols in the later periods.

Among many matrilineal tribes of the North Eastern part of India it is the bride who would set out to marry the groom who would later obtain the surname of the bride after the wedding, on contrary to popular traditions across the globe. The worthiness of the brother of the bride is still a premise of greater noteworthiness than that of her husband in many tribal societies; reminiscence of the primitive matriarchal society when the husband played the second fiddle. Among a few primitive societies in India, the significance of the maternal uncle of the child is still many a fold superior than that of the father's. Many maternal uncles still raise their sister's or their daughter's child. The moon being a female principle is regarded as the maternal uncle or the *chandamama.*

The proto Austroloid Kols retain numerous brother sister legends and songs among themselves which they sing during vital ceremonies. If among the Hindus the eight stars of the Ursa Major is the seven sages and one Arundhati, the wife of one of the seven sages Vashista, then among the Santals the same set of eight stars are seven brothers and one sister Champa.

Like the Hindu brother sister festivals of Bhaiya dooj, Bhai phota, the tribals celebrate Karma which apart from its astronomical significance is also a brother sister festival, a memory of the now forgotten fertility cult. India has diverse primitive customs still practised among different communities and tribes along the vast expanse of the country. Today politics, classical religions along with modern education contribute significantly in doing away with the vibrant heterogeneity of the country. But there are villages which could be islands where many primitive customs still coexist along with the relatively newer ones which could help us unravelling our enigmatic past thereby giving a proper account of our prehistory.

References

1. P.B.Chakravorty, "Monolith memorials of Meghalya" Mar- Aug 93, Himalaya Today.
2. Van Exim. The Religious System of the Munda Tribe. Catholic Press, Ranchi
3. Terence Meaden. The Secrets of the Avebury Stones. Souvenir Press. London
4. Subhashis Das. Sacred Stones in Indian Civilization. Kaveri Books, New Delhi.
5. Van Exim. The Religious System of the Munda Tribe. Catholic Press, Ranchi
6. Ibid.
7. Asko Parpola. Deciphering the Indus script, Cambridge University Press.

6 THE MALE FEMALE DISPARITY

If one observes profoundly he would find that, a male and a female of the same human species are relatively different from each other. Such dissimilarity is more conspicuous in remote villages and it may apparently appear that both the male and the female belong to two different races. Why is it so? To make sense of this phenomenon one needs to go to a village where women have not really been educated under the present arrangement and modernism has not much caste it sway on the older traditions and where ancient customs are fairly well preserved. Here one can really view this prominent disparity between both the genders.

The females of India particularly those of villages dress traditionally in saris whereas her male counterpart has adopted western dress codes. Talking of customs, traditions and ceremonies; be it childbirth, marriage, death or whatsoever, the womenfolk in the village come together to accomplish the service with the minimum or even no male intervention and most thankfully without a Brahman priest uttering Sanskrit mantras.

Whenever I travel to villages in the dense woods, I do not miss the chance to converse with the females whom I regard as encyclopaedias of our civilization and history. If you need to know a country's past, be taught by them; as all of it lies in their millennia old customs, rituals and wisdom. Listening to these kind of women talk (figure out their speech if you can) I get fascinated as it sends a shiver down my spine as I get this feeling that I am hearing one of the most ancient languages of them all which has changed very less with time.

In rural India, the regional languages usually spoken by the women folks are indisputably more intricate than those of their male counterparts. It can therefore be said with asserting certainty that many old women's diction are nasal and their speech comprise words which are archaic and their accent which are just as old have been brought down from the primitive days of matriarchy therefore is indeed difficult for the modern man to grasp. Numerous words which are used by such females are already phased out in the contemporary tongue of their males who could be speaking the same rural language which is comparatively uncomplicated to comprehend as the intricate words which the females employ in their speech would be evidently missing as such terms are substituted with simpler and common ones; the intonation would be more urban with less or no nasalness. For the new listener both the male and female of the same village may sound as they are conversing in two different languages.

The binding ties among the womenfolk themselves grow more perceptible during ceremonies but much of their confederation lies unseen and unnoticed. Whenever there is a function specifically meant for the women it would be only they who would assemble and accomplish the rites and no males are welcome here.

I still reminisce my marriage days when all the women folk of my neighbourhood gathered for the occasion to implement various rituals of the wedding ceremony and even jointly cook for all. The men folks preferred to stay out of these; remarking jokingly all these to be "women's affairs". So strong is their unity that they are even known to share secret sexual fertility rituals. I am aware of at least one such practice where married women on a particular day (I do not remember which) would throng in groups to each other's homes and would then encircle a particular married woman of the house in such a manner so that the activity within gets obstructed from outside and which makes it easy for them to perform the hidden ritual. The main leader would then shove the protruded part of the '*belna*' or the 'roti' roller superficially over the sari upon the vulva of the women and the rest would clap and sing in unison. There are many similar clandestine fertility rites among the rural women folks which are dying off with the onslaught of modernisation, without being documented.

In ancient India women were believed to have conversed in Prakrit. At Nushu in olden China, the women too had a private language of their own. In Japan too certain faction of women also possessed similar secret and private languages. Literature is also known to have been composed in such languages. The Inca women too are believed to have enjoyed a confidential speech too. The prime motive behind such secret languages was that despite being specifically meant for the females, it was primarily to ward off the males out of their privacy. Even in historical India, there are evidences of the use of separate speeches of women. Avanti is supposed to be one such speech.[1] Prakrit too as notified above was a language believed to have been spoken only by the females in India. The use of such private or secret languages by women among themselves until about a century ago positively indicates to an unknown part of human history. It could be that many of these dialects of such village women were infact the languages of the entire tribe once spoken when the entire society was matriarchal during hoary antiquity.

When the social order changed, a patriarchal and patrilineal form of social order set in. The women folk resisted major changes in their lifestyle and preferred retaining their ancient approach to life which contained many archaic fertility rites of the now obsolete matriarchal social order.

The male's life style under such conditions transformed and so did their vernacular, as they were accepting the abundant changes in the world; a world which they would soon be dominating. The alteration of male's lingo came also perhaps with their exposure to other communities speaking different languages.

In the newly transformed world arrangement where male authority has been amplified in all spheres, the females have fashioned a grouping among them, conscientiously safeguarding their millennia old culture and language repudiating any change ushered in by the new male dominated world. In such a scenario the women have retained the primitive vernacular; perhaps for this their language in due course of time has been understood as a secret speech by the newer generations speaking the modern version of the same language.

Worship or puja, which was chiefly a woman's domain once, as discussed in an earlier chapter, is now conducted by the male Brahmin priests pronouncing Sanskrit mantras. Although the daily worshipping in the domestic shrines is still done by women but during ceremonial 'pujas' it is the man who completely dominates the events; the woman is pushed into anonymity.

However, in the village shrines where sacred stones, trees or groves are ritualistically worshipped, it is the male tribal/dalit priest known as *pahans*, *bhakats*, *naikes* etc. who perform the rituals. Earlier the female priests called *bhaktins* would conduct the rituals in such rural temples. The ancient and simple customs once accomplished by the women folk has now begun to be conducted by the male Brahmin priests; the relevance of the female in such 'pujas' has begun to diminish considerably.

In the Hindi heartland Vat Savitri (Pl.6), Chat, Teej, Jeetiya etc are a few festivals which are still performed by the women folks. As a result of the ongoing Aryanisation, Brahmins today have stepped in with their Sanskrit Mantras even in the few remaining female conducted ceremonies shoving the female predominance in such rituals and 'pujas' to the rear (Pl.7). Brahmanisation of these primitive festivals has completely altered the ancient rituals and the primeval quintessence of the ceremony is now vanished altogether. That these ceremonies were conducted precisely by the females till about a few years ago suggest that these traditions have been handed down to current times from the much olden days of the fertility cult when women were dominant in the much ancient sedantric society. Such acculturation today is evidence how fast the last remaining vestiges of this primitive civilization too will fade away with time.

Many village markets still reveal the women hegemony; it is they who are still the prime vendors (Pl.58) which indicate that this occurrence is remnant of a society which had once held the females in a privileged position. In many villages, long rows of women of all ages (particularly married) can still be seen heading towards rivers, ponds or wells; singing unanimously to conduct ceremonies and rituals related either to birth, marriage or death without any intervention of any male priest and any Sanskrit mantras. Such sights which pleases one from the eye to the soul are becoming scarcer by the day is confirmation of the wrapping up of the dominance of females in our society. Such primitiveness of our country though breathing its last is still preserved among these so-called poverty-stricken women of rural India. The soft spoken, humble, and submissive women folk of the villages who still retain the qualities of the forgotten matriarchal societies of the distant past are the last prototypes whose predecessors once venerated the primeval Mother Goddesses.

Reference

1. P.L.Vaidya. Use of Prakrit Dilaects in Sankrit Dramas. Annals of the Bhandarkar, Oriental Research Institute XXXIII. 1952.

7 Sacred Marriages

For the primitives' the earth was not a just a piece of soil. For them it was alive. It slept, awoke, felt pleasure, pain, got angry and would even shower blessings. It was a Goddess; a mother, who menstruated, became fertile, produced as a woman, and even nurtured them like a mother would do to her siblings. Her splendour and magnificence encouraged the early populace to raise numerous megalithic temples and celebrate her glory.

Sarhul is a major fertility ceremony of the proto austroloid tribals which enlightens this primitive belief still prevalent among the existing tribes. Sarhul celebrates the marriage between the mother earth and the father sky. The festival also celebrates the earth becoming fertile and her event of menstruation which is signalled by the blossoming of the Sal tree (*Shorea robusta*). The blooming therefore signifies that Mother Earth is all set to produce as she is fertile now, hence farming can commence. As the blossoming of the Sal flowers differs from one region to other, so does the ceremony. The celebration is also determined by the various phases of the moon, as in Jharkhand Sarhul begins on the full moon of *Phagun* where as in Bengal it lasts till the full moon of *Vaishakh*[1]. For the tribals Sarhul also beckons the beginning of the New Year.

A similar three day fecundity festival is celebrated by the Hindus in East India known as *Ambabuchi*[2] occurring on or a day later to the Summer Solstice in which the sun travels to the tropic of cancer in the northern hemisphere and is the longest day of the year here. As the sun reaches the farthest during the mid summer sunrise it is supposed to be in it fullest fury and the sunrays are believed to fertile the Mother Earth on Ambabuchi days.

Much similar to that in Sarhul during Ambabuchi Mother Earth is also believed to menstruate as these three days are her lean days therefore on these days she should neither be tilled nor heavy objects be dropped on the ground as such actions might inflict pain upon her. Three days later the Mother Earth becomes fertile hence gets ready to be ploughed. Summer Solstice is therefore also related to the enhancement of the fertility of the earth. One fertility custom among the Oraons is just before the Sarhul festival where the dormitory boys are carried by the dhumkuria mahatos to a place far away from the village where they apply red earth on their bodies; which is remnant of their fertility cult days as red is the symbol of fertility and impregnation. Thereafter they are instructed to spit inside a slit of a Sal (*Shorea robusta*) sapling and insert their phallus into it, as the tree here is symbolical of a female.[3]

Megaliths too demonstrate many fertility observances by generating sacred union with the landscape which many scholars deem as sacred marriages[4]. The alignments of megaliths with the landscape are superb renditions of union between the megaliths and the hills in the horizon. Judging by the positioning of the primitive megaliths it can be adduced that the spots where these primitive shrines are located were very particularly selected by the primitive megaliths makers. The landscape was required to be ringed with hills as without them megaliths could not have been raised.

Hills are as enigmatic as the megaliths themselves. In nearly all the religions across the world hills have played a foremost part. It was on the summit of a mountain did Moses receive his commandments, it was upon such a hill Jesus too obtained his sermon; the Jaina tirthankaras from Neminatha to Mahavira received their arihanta on hills. And it was to these hills the primitive megalith makers aligned their megaliths; a deed which can be still be perceived and relished. Hills therefore are the hub of spiritual energy and early man was able to grab their secret significance very long ago[5].

Hills in India are gendered as 'pahar' or 'pahari'; male or female hills respectively. A triangular hill having its apex pointing upwards being phallic in its representation is a male hill. But hills possessing 'V' indentations are symbolical of the female vagina or hills with rounded peaks are figurative of the Mother's breasts which render both the types as 'pahari' or she-hills.

Pregnancy being a major feature of the obsolete fertility cult of the yesteryears, a hill resembling a reclining woman may also comprise of a bloated middle which matches the pregnant belly of a recumbent woman was a very popular image of the recumbent Mother Goddess form all over the world during ancient times. The Zulzul pahari (Pl.51) is a unique archetype of such a form with a pregnant abdomen and having even a "V" type cleft, which is actually a triangle with its vertex towards the bottom; is the female vaginal representation.

Many megaliths are aligned to male triangular hills. The huge Purni Mandar megalithic complex is positioned in alignment to three triangular hills. The menhirs here face the Winter Solstice sunrise and to their opposite is the triangular Tilra Hill in the far horizon at whose backside the sun sets in the Summer Solstice. To the right is the triangular Harhad Hill and to the left of the megaliths is the triangular Sultana Hill. These enjoinment of hills and megaliths by way of alignments propose primarily that the megaliths are female shrines and that such alignments of the megaliths to the triangular male hills are the consecrated communion or 'sacred marriage' between them.

The ancient megaliths are regarded as female shrines; therefore their enjoinments to the triangular hills symbolical of male principles signify the theory of the sacred marriages being accomplished between the both. The dolmen in the North Western gradient of the Bengwa Pahari which translates to 'the frog she-hill' discovered by Faiyaz Ahmed (Pl.13) demonstrates a remarkable union between the ancient monument and a triangular male hill in the distant horizon. This dolmen has two turtle shelled capstones resting on two large natural boulders with a wide gap in the middle below the capstones having openings on its either sides. The tomb opens up towards the triangular hill of Janhe at 210 deg and between these is a rock cluster which houses a ceremonial 'yoni' quite similar to that of Jabra Road. This alignment surely demonstrates the sacred anion of both the principles.

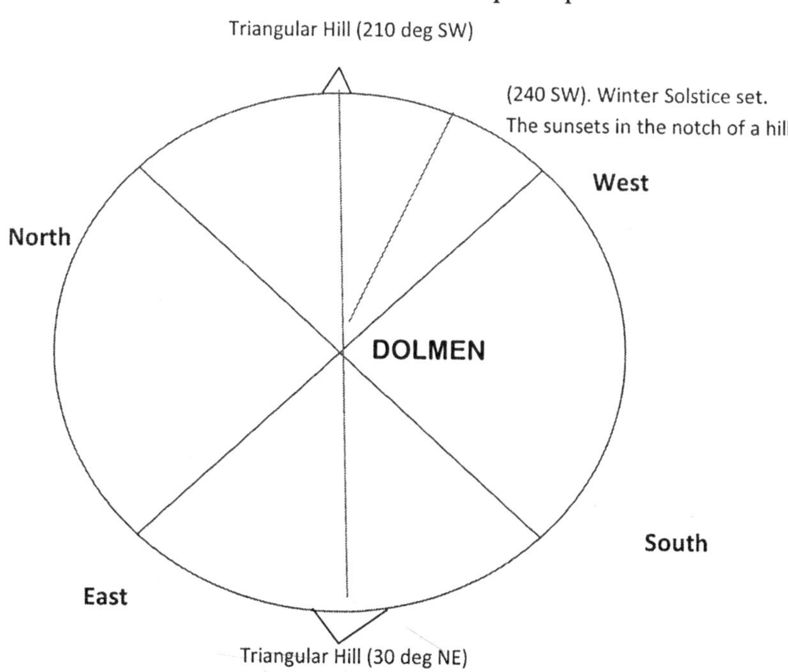

Fig. 1. THE BENGWA PAHAR DOLMEN.
The Megalith is at the middle of the circle.
The either sided openings of the shrine are aligned to hills in the landscape.

This opening faces the Winter Solstice sunset where the sun slips into a "V" notch in a hill in the distant horizon. Such an orientation certainly beckons toward the sacred union between the female shrine and the male triangular hill. The other side of the dolmen's opening is oriented towards 30 deg NE.

Villagers have excavated many funerary urns from the tomb below the capstones of which a few is even believed to have revealed coins belonging to the times of Shah Alam of early 19th century, suggesting the burial rites have been continuing inside the sacred cove to very recent times since the ancient periods. A frog or '*beng*' (in the local dialect) shaped memorial dolmen near the earlier megalith has perhaps lent its name to the hill. Faiyaz however informs me that the hill is also known as the Palebhari pahari. The word 'pal' is of an unknown origin but the rustic villagers still use the term for impregnation, whereas 'bhar' could either imply to the archaic fertility Goddess Var or to the filling up (of the womb) indicative of pregnancy. Therefore evident by its name its apparent that the hill was in concomitance with the ancient fertility cult .

One Hindu ceremony which comes to my mind is the Maha Shivaratri in which Lord Shiva is believed to marry his consort Parvati. N.K.Rao, writer and the former Professor of Indian Institute of Astrophysics, Bangalore informs me that Shivaratri occurs every month one day before the new moon. But in the Maha Shivaratri which transpires once every year, the moon on the 14th lunar day comes closest to the rising sun in the east. This is the imagery of Shiva's marriage to Parvati. One is supposed to witness this rare astronomical spectacle keeping awake the night.

References

1. Ram Dayal Munda. Adi Dharma- Religious beliefs of the Adivasis of India. Sarini. Bhubaneswar.
2. Subhashis Das. Sacred Stones in Indian Civilization. Kaveri Books.
3. Vinita Damodaran. Gender, Forests and Famine in 19th Cent Chotanagpur, India. Indian Journal of Gender Studies.
4. Terence Meaden. Stonehenge The secret of the solstice, Souvenir.
5. Subhashis Das. Sacred Stones in Indian Civilization. Kaveri Books.

8 TRIANGLES

It is strange why stone triangles, both the isosceles and the equilateral type were placed either in the middle or at the side of megaliths. I have not observed such triangles inside a megalithic complex any where else other than in Hazaribagh (Pl.8), but I know very well, there ought to be many around, waiting to be discovered. The triangle is a geometrical shape and geometry was known to humanity thousands of years even prior to the birth of megalithism. But the shape must have had a representative significance in their beliefs neither they shouldn't have been planting them within their shrines.

Triangles were sexual representations also; as discussed in a former chapter, the ones with their vertex to their top were symbolical of the male organ where as the reverse type as that of the female vulva. The "V" feature as we have seen earlier is the up turned triangle; representative of the female sexual organ. Apart from these, triangles with pointed tops can apparently perform as pointers too. Studying a few of the megaliths I identified that these triangles were certainly performing as such. The megaliths of Purni Mandar, Banadag, Jabra Road, Birbir , Rola and Lati contain one or more triangles in each and all are aligned towards significant sunrises and sets, meaning, they were planted there to execute the job of pointers. The Birbir and Lati triangles point towards the sunrises of the Equinox and Winter solstice mornings respectively. Rola which has three triangles of comparative sizes points towards not only to the Winter Solstice sunrise but another pointer is oriented towards the sunset on the Summer Solstice evenings and the largest triangle is made to indicate the Kanhari Hill (Pl.56).

If stone circles were assumed to be the womb or the vulva of the Great Mother, the location of the phallic triangles in the centre of the circles as that in Banadag were possibly representation of the divine copulation (Pl.9). Such designs were perhaps the precursors to the much later evolved Shiva Linga and Parvati Yoni symbols. The Purni Mandar megalithic site has about six different megalithic complexes spread over a whopping area of more than a kilometre. One of these sites have a single menhir with a triangular tip; which is the largest directional pointer of Rola. However, on contrary to the Rola pointer, this triangle is aligned towards the mid winter sunrise. The Birbir megalithic complex has a solitary isosceles triangle which points towards to the due east (Pl.51).

The tiny triangle in the Pacahi Baba megalith of Jabra Road is a stunner. The minuscule triangle sits pretty peeping out of the earth pointing to the heavens above (Pl.10), positioned on the alignmental line between the Kanhari and the Bawanwey hills on its either sides. The wedge shaped triangle is placed at the centre of one Rola type pointer at its back and another middle sized menhir with a tapered top at the front which in turn is oriented to the Zulzul hill at 150 deg SE. There are no doubts on contrary to its size this triangle must have been of great magnitude to the primitives for it seems to have been designed for an unknown yet a specific purpose.

However Terence Meaden does mention[1] pyramidal stones (which should be the triangles which I speak of) in the middle of the Harestone Down megaliths of UK whose photographs are definitely startlingly similar to the centrepiece triangular megaliths of Hazaribag! That megaliths were once and are still associated with sorcery is well known but it could also be connected to Tantra. In the very primitive non-Aryan Tantra too triangles were sexual icons. That both megaliths and Tantra is non-Aryan in origin and both are related with the Goddess worship therefore such a bond cannot be spurned. The sudden find of an equilateral stone near the tall pole like megaliths in Khunti indicates that the artefact may have had a ritualistic importance (Pl.27).

A question certainly rises whether these triangles have a geometrical connexion too? Different people have different ideas in regards to the origin of mathematics. A few of them ascribe the Vedic fire altar to it which could be true but the fact of the matter is that arithmetic, geometry and even astronomy were known to people much, much prior to the Vedic times. Megaliths as those of Punkri Barwadih, Hanamsagar, Bodhayan Shila, Nilurallu and Vishwa Shila of Jagannath Pahari are demanding confirmations of prevalence of mathematics in hoary antiquity as all these are remains of this enigmatic civilization.

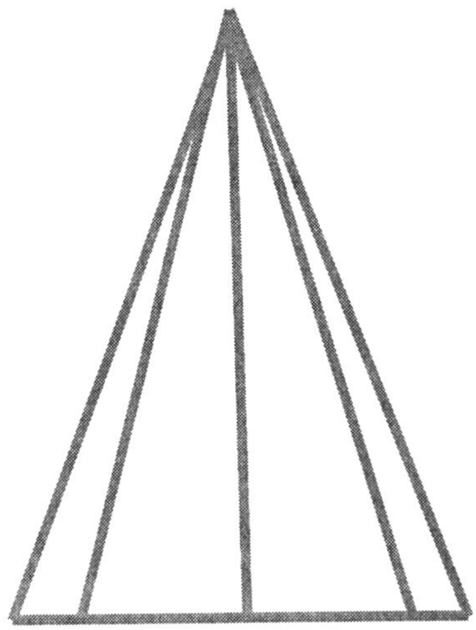

Fig. 2.
This is how these two triangles appear in the Rock art of Isko

Triangles as motifs have been used profusely in various Indian art. In rock arts triangles can date back to the Palaeolithic times. Isko rock art in, Hazaribagh presents a brilliant example of numerous geometrical motifs in which triangles feature prominently. The above sketch of two triangles was found in Panel - 1 in Isko.

The primitives refrained from revealing their dreams to others, it is alleged that they articulated their dreams and feelings through abstract symbols of geometrical forms and designs by drawing or engraving them either on small stone pieces or on cave walls.[2] Harappan potteries from Amri, Kalibangan Mehrgarh, Nal , Kuli have revealed numerous triangles either painted or incised. Terracotta triangular cakes have been discovered in Harappan cities[3]. The motifs on the potsherds have been usually found to be coloured and outlined with rows of horizontal lines. Triangles have also been found in lines with circular dots in the spaces between the triangles.[4]. The problem is whether painted triangles and megalithic triangles meant the same. In the Indus valley, triangles have been collected from anywhere; from the fire altars, streets and even from the latrines. Triangles in its true self or as its motif might have served diverse purposes but no one knows the precise rationale of the artefact but it can be understood these triangles must have been of immense value to the megalithic folks, the Harappans as it were for the cave men of the Palaeolithic era.

Why do the megaliths of Rola have three, Banadag and Jabra Road two triangles each and Birbir, Lati and Purni Mandar house one triangle apiece we do not have any clue? Rola is puzzling as it also houses a phallus apart from the male triangles. If triangles are symbols of phalluses why then they also placed a stone phallus in the same site?

References

1. Terence Meaden: The Secrets of the Avebury Stones. Souvenir.
2. Subhashis Das. Sacred Stones in Indian Civilization. Kaveri Books.
3. Joseph Manuel. A Note on the enigmatic Triangular Terracotta Cakes. Purattatva 37, 2006-07.
4. Anisha Saxena. A study of early Harappan Pottery Motifs. Purattatva 35. 2004-05.

9 The Enigmatic Primitive Symbols

Every auspicious celebration here from pregnancy to death and all the various in-betweens as births and marriages etc are calendar centric which are based on astronomy. Rivers and hills were consigned with celestial names in remote antiquity and in many places they are still maintained. I hardly know any other place other than India where astronomy still plays such a central role in their people's lives. Neither am I aware of any other place where people keep their names on geometrical symbols and structures, constellations and stars. Below is given a few of such names among the many:

Human names (mathematical)	Meaning
• Golu, Britta	Circle
• Golak	Sphere
• Tribhuj, Trikon	Triangle
• Chaturbhuj	Rectangle
• Shanku	Cone
• Rekha	Line
• Nishan	Sign
• Prateek	Symbol
Names (astronomical)	**English equivalent**
• Sonu, Sonua	
• Hatiya	Denevola
• Kanya	Virgo
• Arar /Adra	Orion

• Soti, Swati	Spica
• Saptarshi	Great Bear (Ursa major)
• Dhruv	Pole star
• Rohit	---
• Vishakha	Arctuarus
• Chitra	Corvi
• Sravan	Spica
• Bishu/Vishu	The Equinox
• Uttara	Sagittari/Pegasi/Leonis
• Rohini	Pleiades
• Anuradha	Librae
• Mithun	Gemini
Ayan	The sun's passage towards both the solstices
. Dakhshinayan	The course of the sun from Summer Solstice to the Winter solstice.
. Uttarayan	The course of the sun from the Winter solstice to Summer Solstice

Formerly many rural children were named, according to the days of the week on which they were born, as:

Names	In English
• Somra (The moon)	Monday
• Mangal, Mangra (Mars)	Tuesday
• Budhan, Budhwa, Budhna (Mercury)	Wednesday
• Biru, Birhat, Brihaspat (Jupiter)	Thursday
• Sukhra, Sukhi, Bhora, Bhiru (Venus)	Friday
• Sanichar, Sanichara (Saturday)	Saturday
• Ravi, Itu, Itwari , Iti (The Sun)	Sunday

(My mother's pet name is Itu; the sun God, whose worship is still conducted by the Bengalis in Eastern India)

Apart from this, the males are known to suffix the term "Chandra" or the moon as their central names. Therefore enjoining the name Chandra to the main names as

Ram, Mohan or Deepak converts them into Ramchandra, Mohanchandra or Deepakchandra et al, testimony of their lineage to the moon in their olden times.

Close to Patna (ancient Patliputra, one of the ancient most cities of the world) is the town Khagol which literally means 'astronomy'. In close proximity there is also a town called Taregana which once translated into English would mean "Singing the stars" or "The song of the stars". Aryabhatt, the renowned mathematician and astronomer held to have been born in 476 AD in Kusumpur, a village adjoining Patna is assumed to be associated with Taregana.

Near Hazaribagh, my hometown is the amazing mathematical and astronomical site of the Jagannath Pahari built at some unknown period by some unknown people. Just adjacent to it there is a small village called Meru which in Puranic literature means the Poles. A neighbouring village is oddly called Danda. Now combining the names of both the villages gives rise to the astronomical Meru-Danda which literally means either the spinal cord or the axis of the world!

All these are evidences that mathematics, astronomy and astrology is still a way of life here since ancient period.

Symbols

Symbols are an integral part of the human evolution; the ancient world was full of it. Dreams they say were not expressed candidly but through symbols, therefore the rock art motifs are believed to be conceptual expressions visualised in dreams or in trance under the influence of some intoxication.

The first drawings of humanity must have been the very primitive tattoos which still vaguely exist in many ancient countries as that of India. These comprising various geometrical patterns and designs like zigzags, parallels, waves, bangles, criss-crosses and so on like as today were made on the skins of the ancients (Pl.62). Tattoos worn chiefly by women may also have been done for fecundity purposes. Today of course, this art is fast dying but whatever left is done merely as a tradition; its denotation lost with time. Abstract cave arts too had more or less similar designs as the zigzags, criss-crosses, triangles, circles, spirals and so on ones found in tattoos (Pl.63).

The red colour used in the rock arts all over could indicate to the menstrual blood hence designate fertility implications. In years to come Harappan pottery would contain the same icons along with other flora and fauna motifs. Horizontal parallel lines with diamond patterns, criss- crosses, parallelograms with criss-crosses, V patterns, spirals and circles can also be seen on Harappan pottery[1].

Near similar designs would re-emerge in the Chalcolithic and Iron Age megalithic potteries[2]. Relatively similar designs combining with the later evolved symbols can be seen on the walls of the mud huts of villages today painted during festivals as the Sohrai which the scholars advocate as fertility motifs. In primitive Tantra, symbols being mandatory to accomplish the rituals are acquired by the movements of the fingers as shown in the illustration (Pl.15). Talking of the abstract geometrical designs in the rock arts, there aren't many apposite explanations of them. One line of thought interprets that many of the primitive hunting scenes could be symbolical; and the arrows or spears being hurled at the game need not be true weapons but spiritual arrows and spears.

Many primitive signs are still being drawn or surfaces of potteries, walls or even on the floors in a continued tradition since the Palaeolithic era and are worshipped in every Hindu household merely as a custom whose meanings are now lost with time. But that many primitive symbols of the ancient world are still in use thousands of miles away from their discovered sites suggests that people were either migrating carrying their ideas and beliefs with them to far-flung lands or these symbols had a universal understanding, usage and beliefs.

The below stated primitive symbol (Fig.3) has been found in many rock art sites across the world as in Chevot of France is surprisingly still being used profusely in Hindu rituals which may testify to the above hypothesis. This icon is still precisely drawn in red as in the archaic rock arts though is sketched today on walls, earthen or brass water pots during marriages.

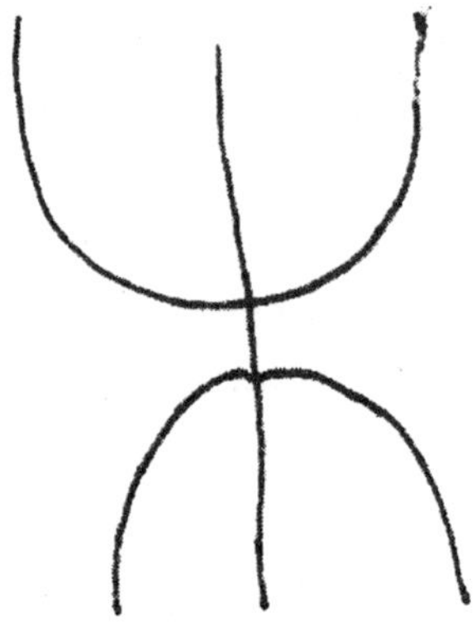

Fig. 3.
This sacred fertility symbol found in various rock arts as that in Chevot of France are still in use in India during Hindu marriages and is also drawn on water pitchers.

The below illustrated design (Fig.4) of concentrated circles with a dot in its centre found in many primitive rock arts across the world is both a Hindu and a tribal symbol. Hindus and tribals draw it on the floor with rice powder or with its semi liquid gruel. Quite similar to the rock arts painted in red the present day Hindus still draw these sacred signs and symbols on walls on water pots (Fig.4) and on many other bodies in red colour by mixing red vermillion (locally known as sindoor) with oil. This symbol (Fig.3) is also found carved on many megaliths across the world like on the fallen stone in Drumtroddan megalithic complex, on the Ballochmyle walls and even on the recumbent stones of Cairnbaan in UK[1]. That this must have been a major auspicious symbol all through antiquity is evident from it being found on so many rock arts and megaliths the world over and it still being used is confirmation to this hypothesis. The noted tribal exponent Ram Dayal Munda believes that this is a very ancient symbol denoting life and human manifestation[2].

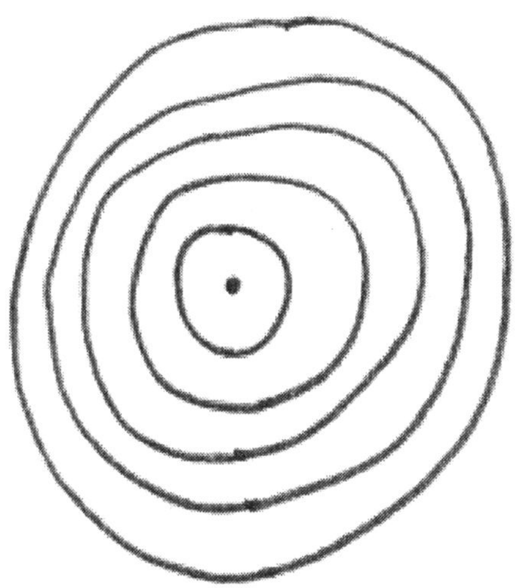

Fig. 4
This symbol is drawn in India on the floor and on the walls of homes, both by the tribals and the Hindus and is even found both in the rock arts and on megaliths across the world.

A spiral of another kind (Fig.5) is still being drawn as design in arippans, alponas, sohrais and khonds etc in an unbroken manner since antiquity both in the tribal and non tribal tradition.

These spirals drawn both in clockwise or anticlockwise modes are also found in rock arts all over the world and even in the rock paintings of Isco in Hazaribag. The symbols appear on potteries in UK known as the Grooved Ware and even on the megaliths of Newgrange, UK[3], and India. The spiral assumes various shapes and forms and many are even joined with each other as found in many megaliths of UK and even in the golden ornaments of South America.

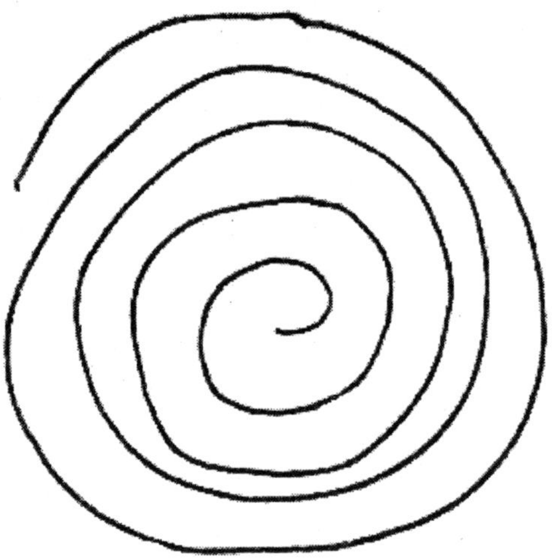

Fig .5

This spiral moves in both clockwise and anticlockwise and can be traced to primitive rock arts to engravings on megaliths all over the world and in India. This design in India is a popular motif made on the floors in rangolis, alponas and khonds etc and even on walls on sohrais.

Though the rituals have changed with times many primitive rock art motifs of our ancestors still continue to live amongst our household in our customs today. Without the study of such primitive signs and symbols, the understanding of the prehistory of a country would remain incomplete; after all such signs are the accounts of these unknown people who go to make a country's history. More efforts should be made to connect the sacred texts as the Puranas and the Vedas with various primitive rituals of both the tribals and the Hindus.

References

1. Tejas Garge. A Note on Sothi Pottery. Purattatva 37. 2006-07
2. V.D.Mishra. Dept of Ancient History, Culture and archaeology. Investigations into the Megalithic Cultures of Allahabad District, Uttar Pradesh
3. Julian Cope. The Modern Antiquarian. Thorsons
4. Ram Dayal Munda. Adi Dharam- Religious beliefs of the Adivasis of India Sarini
5. Christopher Knight and Robert Lomas. Uriel's Machine. Fair Winds Press.

10 MEGALITHS OF ROLA AND SACRED ASTRONOMY

Hills were prerequisites for megaliths, as primitive megaliths in India were not raised without aligning them to hills in the landscape. Therefore, hills were the outer periphery of megaliths without which these primitive temples were incomplete.

Many a times one may find that a few stones in the megalithic complex may not have been aligned towards any hills, if that be the case, it is probable they are oriented towards major sunrises or sets as in Rola where although a few alignments of the stones are towards Kesura, Kanhari and Bawanwey hills but the rest are tilted towards the Summer and Winter Solstice sunrises and sets. Punkri Burwadih, Jagannath Pahari[1], Hanamasagar and Vibhuthihalli[2] all reveal precise alignments towards major sunrises.

Apart from well-defined arrangements for observational and horizon astronomy by the primitive astronomers in such megalithic complexes, Punkree Burwadih and the stone models of Jagannath Pahari[3] disclose profound mathematics too, as discussed in detail in my former book *Sacred Stones in Indian Civilization*. It is noteworthy that such alignments were not the only domains of megaliths but even of ancient temples which have also been found to be laid with mathematical perfection, aligned, and oriented to cardinal points. R.S.Bisht, the ex Joint Director General of Archaeological Survey of India has discovered that even the towns of primitive cities of Indus Valley Civilization as Dholavira were arranged according to mathematics and astronomy[4]. That geometry was engaged in the construction of Harappan cities was also found by Michel Danino, a freelance researcher on Indus valley[5].

On contrary to popular beliefs ancient megalithic complexes like the ones of Punkree Burwadih, Rola, Birbir, were not build arbitrarily at sites where they are today. Years of research has shown me that the primitive megalithic folks would position their megaliths at the intersection of the alignments of hills in the horizon, therefore they hunted for places where there would be hills in the landscape and/or an intersection be possible by way of their alignments so that they would be able to assemble a complex as they desired and a cross in circle be created in the process. The cross in the circle is a highly venerated symbol since the Palaeolithic era. The horizon being circular and megaliths being the omphalos would be positioned on the intersection of the alignments with the hills in the circular horizon thereby completing the cross in the circle. Such alignments and intersections even find mention in the Vishnu Purana. The Vishnu Purana names the intersectional spots as "*sandhi sthal*" which are very sacred spots where the gods makes their *purs.*[6]

The ancients created lot many patterns of stones by aligning and orienting their sacred megalithic burials not only to the hills in the landscapes but even to the major sunrises and sets.

Rola, about 8 kms east of Hazaribagh, is a tiny megalithic complex which may seem very insignificant to the ignorant. I remember seeing the disappointment in the eyes of a retired government archaeologist from Chhattisgarh who visited the site at the behest of the Jharkhand Government along with a busload of students of Ranchi University. He quipped, "Oh this! We have better..."

The poor archaeologist was misinformed as Rola isn't merely '*this*', it is more, much more than just '*this*'. If only the archaeologist knew what treasure this site holds! Rola despite being a primitive tribal *sasandiri* with burial stones could be seen arranged haphazardly is not quite like other megalithic burials; it is unique in many ways. The shrine houses very few stones, a superbly crafted phallus with glans; the only one of its kind I have discovered so far, three stone triangles of comparative sizes and of course a few recumbent stones which are perhaps the burial covers.[7] There is a long reclined stone placed on an East West orientation which has cupules carved on it. As for these cupules or cupmarks believed to be symbols of the Mother Goddess the stone could be deemed as a female stone. Female stones are not unknown in megalithic culture around the world.

The Khasis in Meghalaya regard reclined stones to be female as they were laid in honour of "*Ka-Yobai*", the primeval omnipotent Mother Goddess.[8] Among the Angami Nagas the recumbent stones on the ground are female principles and the 'erect stone' represents the male. With the Kacha Nagas, the dolmens are female stones[9]. In Madagascar too the concept of male and female stones amidst megaliths is still quite popular[10].

As the vermillion, a symbol of fertility is donned by married women in India sacred stones and menhirs are similarly marked with vermilion elevating such stones as not only being sacred but also because these are female deities.

Sacred alignments in Rola

My former book "*Sacred Stones in Indian Civilization*" had perspicuously stated how our very own ancient mathematical and astronomical text 'Surya Siddhanta' talks of alignments of cities in the ancient times. The book states that the *madhyarekha* or the axis of the earth which connects the poles passes through Kurukhshetra, and the cities of Rohitak and Ujjyani[11].

Let us now look into a few of the orientations and alignments of Rola (Pl.55) and awe at their astonishing understanding, knowledge and meticulous planning of the primitive megalith makers with which they raised this momentous monument. Standing at the centre of the shrine one can observe that the monument is placed on the alignment between the Bawanwey and the Kesura hills at 200 degrees West of South and 40 degrees East of North respectively.

Of the three triangular pointers of comparative sizes, the bigger one is positioned to point at the Kanhari hill to an azimuth of about 320 deg North of West. The remaining two smaller triangular pointers however do not point towards any hill but seem to be astronomical stones, evident from their positioning; as the smaller one indicates towards 120 degree SE; the approximate azimuth of the Winter Solstice at this latitude.

The larger one points to the sunset of the Summer Solstice at 300 NW.

The largest pointer uniting with the larger triangle has been oriented towards the summer solstice sunrise (Pl.56) from behind the left slope of the Silwar hill.

One conventional alignment can be observed standing just at the rear of the tall inclined pointed menhir where one can see this stone and the phallus is placed in straight line to the triangular Kesura hill.

The cup marked recumbent female megalith has been laid with a tidy and a simple east-west orientation (Pl.57). The slim tipped eastern end of this recumbent stone serves as a cursor to indicate the magnetic east at a cluster of stones atop the right flank of the Silwar Hill. A raised stone here on this part of the hill has been inclined towards due south.

Rola never ceases to marvel as how much in-depth planning was induced by the primitives to create amazing visuals by sagacious alignments. Touching the phallus, passing through the gap between the two triangles and intersecting the East West recumbent stone the North-South axis of the site eventually merges with the "V" feature on the right flank of the Zulzul Hill in the horizon at the South of the megalithic complex. Stooping low on this North-South axis one can view the phallus 'fitting snugly' on the vaginal "V" of the hill signifying the accomplishment of the copulation with the female hill. Such a merger of the phallus to the "V" cleft of the Recumbent Mother Goddess form of the Zulzul pahari is also demonstrated in Birbir.

The "V" since hoary antiquity as discussed in an earlier chapter is actually the symbol of the female vulva[12]. This sacred union of the stone phallus of Rola or Birbir and the vulvar "V" of the Goddess hill though not heard prior to this was certainly a component of the now extinct fertility cult of the much ancient times. This view in Rola today is obstructed by the construction of an eye sore; a poultry farm in between the hill and the megalith.

Squatting at a particular point on the North-South axis of the monument and gazing towards the Goddess Hill one can obtain this stunning view of the two triangles on the either side 'framing' the recumbent 'female' stone while the phallus gracefully 'lifts' the stone from her centre (Pl.54).

This act can be conjectured as a symbolic union between the phallus and the female stone. A trifle drift from the exact location spoils the view!

The Mathematics of Rola

This spectacular view of the framing the horizontal stone by the two opposite sided triangles on the North-South axis (Pl.54) could only have been derived by the precise arrangements and alignment of the stones. The megalith makers' knowledge of equals, halves and doubles along with the understanding of ratios were a few prerequisites to produce this spectacle.

Measuring the distances of the stones on the North-South axis we find that the length between the decumbent stone and the middle of the gap of the two triangles is equal to the length between the triangles and the phallus. The distance from the viewing point of the framing of the recumbent stone to the phallus is also equal to the length from the phallus to the triangles which is conversely identical from the triangles to the fallen menhir. In other words the four positions between the female stone to the framing point have been positioned in equal halves.

The length between the recumbent menhir and the larger pointer has been made equal to the distance between the menhir and the central point in the gap between the triangles. The distance between the phallus and the pointer is approximately double the stretch between menhir and the pointer which is identical to the lengths between the menhir and the phallus. The arrangements of the rest of the stones in Rola give evidence that the stones in many ancient megalithic complexes as that of Rola are also not arbitrarily placed but have been positioned employing precise scheduling and measurement.

All these dramatic arrangements seem to me as fascinating pieces of primitive engineering, how could they do this? As to do all of these they had to be reasonably knowledgeable as mathematicians, astronomers and landscapers something which does not seem plausible at such ancient times. The engineering and the artwork was achieved by the primitive astronomer-priests discreetly studying the landscape and the hills visible from this spot. The horizon around Rola is unusually ringed with hills which made the spot a natural selection for the astronomer-priests. Was choosing the spot a coincidence that the hex sectioning becomes so remarkably conspicuous from the megaliths or did they just stumble on to it? I asked Antony Roper Crerar, the celebrated archaeoastronomer from UK who was helping me in my research since many years now and had also visited Rola a few years ago.

This is an extract of his answer in his email, "*...and congratulations on Rola identifying. Yes, I should have been more alert when I was there.... There is so much going on in your neck of the woods and I was so astonished at the similarity to the British experience that I did not do a longer scrutiny of your sites.*

..now you should repeat this approach with PB (this is the megaliths of Punkree Burwadih) and any other stone which has a clear aspect in your region.... You are amazed at the establishment of this site and wonder if they 'stumbled' on it...or had calculated the position before...?...Nooo Subhashis...they were looking for it...they undoubtedly recognised the significance of your latitude for allowing hex-sectioning of the circle..and possibly, if they came from elsewhere, had predicted this situation and calculated where to find it by long experience from establishment of other alignments in territories to the north or south of you. The trained astronomer would immediately recognise the potential of the Rola plain ringed by mountains when walking into it on a clear day and indeed, might have been actively searching for it".

They were indeed great astronomers and mathematicians, something not expected from them... fine, but the question still remains why on earth all this geometry and astronomy? I presume it was the once venerated fertility cult and the Great Goddess which inspired them into astronomy, mathematics and geometry.

Cupules

Rounded engravings made on stones labelled as cupules or cupmarks as many scholars hold are symbols of the great Goddesses' womb or the genitals[13] representation of the primordial Mother Goddess.

Such rounded cupmarks, as I have noticed can be found engraved randomly on horizontal stone surfaces in a megalithic site and are today regarded as rock art[14]. The other type is the two rowed eight in each cupule making a total of sixteen of them all. These are smaller circular engravings as compared to the ones of the other kind. The two-rowed eight in each cupmarks are made by village children today to play a game with small pebbles known with varied names as 'goti', 'chausa', 'diggam' etc.

However, chances are that such sixteen cupules found on many megaliths may have been brought down from a more primitive source when such cavities were probably used as the so called 16-month calendars and pebbles (Pl.16) and were implements for counting other than being Mother Goddess symbols. Strangely unlike in other countries cupmarks in India is generally found on horizon stones.

Portholes have been found on both vertical and horizontal stones in India. Single circular holes have been found at the middle of megaliths from UK to India . Alexander Thom is believed to have had designed a 16-month megalithic calendar which has been researched to find that the calendar works fairly successfully in UK.

But then can a calendar intended for primitive England could be functional in remote India? Why not, if so many megalithic architectures can be found to be common in these two distant lands, if megaliths are dubbed with the identical name of 'sasan' both in Jharkhand and in distant UK and furthermore if Thom's megalithic yard can also found to be operational in South-Indian megalithic architectures, then the now extinct sixteen-month megalithic calendar discovered by Thom must have been a worldwide phenomenon, hence prevalent here even in India. At a later chapter, we would look into how much was common between the megalithic calendars of prehistoric India and UK.

References

1. Subhashis Das. Sacred Stones in Indian Civilization. Kaveri Books.
2. N.Kameshhara Rao and Priya Thakur The astronomical significance of megalithic stone alignments at Vibhuthihalli in Northern Karnataka. Journal of Astronomical History and Heritage)
3. Subhashis Das. Sacred Stones in Indian Civilization. Kaveri Books.
4. T.S. Subramaniun. The Rise and Fall of a Harappan City. Frontline. Jun 18 2010, "The city of Dholavira.... followed a resolute set of principles of planning and architecture with mathematical precision and perhaps with astronomically established orientations."
5. Michel Dannino. Dholavira's Geomtery: A Preliminary Study. Purattatva 35 2004-2005)
6. Vishnu Purana 11nd ansh . IInd chapter, 46-49

7. Subhashis Das. Sacred Stones in Indian Civilization. Kaveri Books.
8. J.H.Hutton. The meaning and Method of the erection of Monoliths by the Naga Tribes. The Journal of the Royal Anthropological Institute of Great Britain and Ireland. Vol II, 1922.
9. P.B.Chakravorty, “Monolith memorials of Meghalya” Mar- Aug 93 Himalaya Today.
10. Julian Cope. The Modern Antiquarian. Thorsons
11. A.K.Chakravarty. The Surya Siddanta. The Asiatic Society.
12. Subhashis Das. Sacred Stones in Indian Civilization
13. Ibid.
14. James Woodford. Unearthed Austraila’s Lost civilization. The Sydney Morning herald News review. Sept, 21, 1996.

11 Megalithic Astronomy and Alignments

The testimony of the ancient people's wisdom in astronomy and mathematics in the archaic megaliths stands in stark contradiction to what we have been told by the scholars that the megalithic folks were little more than just barbaric people if not complete savages. But then, you see, savages do not know ratios, hex sectioning, value of pi, neither do they multiply, divide, do complex mathematics nor even they know the exact sunrise points and dates of many significant days other than those of the Equinoxes, Summer and Winter Solstices and even those of the solstices of the moon. Not to forget the three inscribed lines on the Viswa Shila, which unambiguously illustrates the Equator, the Tropics of Cancer, Capricorn, and their angles!

Many menhirs of the proto austroloid tribals have been found facing towards the Winter Solstice sunrise, is another instance of their penchant towards astronomy.

For the Hindus, Winter Solstice known as uttarayán is celebrated on the makar sankranti day of 14/15th January. On this day the ingress of the sun occurs into the zodiac of Capricorn (makara in Sanskrit) from Sagittarius (Dhanu). According to the Sanskrit calendar the transition of the sun also denotes the shortest day and the sun's northward journey. So vital is this day that many melas or fairs across India as the Kumbha Mela commences from this day of the uttarayan. Holy dips in many sacred rivers become an essentiality on this day across the country.

Many a thousand years ago the uttarayan or the Winter Solstice was believed to have been commemorated on the real dates of the Winter Solstice i.e on 22/23 Dec in place of the currently established 14th Jan, which would mean that the fairs ought to have commenced from 22/23 Dec.

About a thousand year ago as a result of the precession of the equinoxes the date of the ingress of the sun into the Capricorn was believed to be on about 30/31st December and today the date has been pushed farther to the 14th January. A near similar alteration of about 22/23 days too has occurred even in the Vernal Equinox. Today according to Hindu calendars the Vernal Equinox known as the *mahavishuv* to Hindus is celebrated on 14th April. Communities as the Bengalis, Punjabis celebrate their new years on or around this day which also is the beginning date of their respective calendars.

One such site among thousand others where a Makar Sankranti fair is held every year is the eminent Hathia Pathaar site in Phusro, on the banks of the sacred Damodar River near Bokaro Steel City (Pl.43). The Hathia Pathaar[1] already attended to at length in my former book, I believe would be redundant to be discussed in here. The motive to bring up the site in this context is to draw the readers' attention towards the astounding natural straight and long paralleled line formations of stones which strangely have orientations of around 130 deg South of East and 300 North of West which are the estimated azimuths of the Winter Solstice sunrise and the Summer Solstice sunset (Pl.44 & Pl.45)!

The river has numerous parallel stone rows which and as well as the Hathia Pathar (Pl.45) itself along with the long stone row in question are oriented to these azimuths.

But the site however raises more questions than answers. How can nature be so perfect to create such an alignment towards the mid-winter sunrise and the mid summer sunset? The primitives must have learnt of the site's bearings by observation. Deep admiration does arise for them as the moment they may have spotted the site, the idea of the azimuths may have emerged on their minds which they may have had authenticated by astute scrutiny. The site hence proposes the truth that the primitives were always in look out for orientations towards sunrises, sets and cardinal points. The site is a natural site naturally aligned to the winter solstice. Here fairs are still held on Makar Sankranti days.

But the reason that these stone rows have a winter solstice orientation must have made this site incredibly sacred for the ancients therefore it must have become a place of natural choice for them to celebrate the Winter Solstice by holding Makar Sankranti melas here since very ancient times. The site presumably confirms that the fair of Makar Sankranti (Uttarayan) was probably celebrated here when the sun rose at an approximate 130 deg during the Winter Solstice it still does in the same azimuth. The change in the Winter Solstice dates in India to 14th Jan also had the mela (fair) pushed to 14th January.

As for the adivasis having their menhirs orientated towards the mid-winter sunrises were perhaps based on the lesser-known bone burial ceremony of the Mundas called

Jang-topa which was observed around the winter solstice. The bones of the deceased would be buried on this day and they would erect a menhir in the departed's memory facing the Winter Solstice sunrise; the day of raising the monument. Munda tribes of different regions held this ritual either on the months of Pus or Magh[2] in December or January respectively, in other words around the usual Winter Solstice or the day of Makar Sankranti. This demonstrates that even the tribals convene this bone burial rite in both the original and the changed dates of the Winter Solstice. Maghe Parob is another among the numerous other ceremonies of the tribals conducted around the mid winter sunrise. Mundas speaking the Naguri Mundari celebrate the festival in January on the Makar Sankranti day, where as the Mundas who speak the Hansdaya Mundari would celebrate the occasion on December[3] perhaps around the Winter Solstice.

That many primitive monuments across the world are oriented towards the mid winter sunrise confirms that the megaliths too belonged to this unfathomable primitive civilisation. Chances are that these civilizations too had more or less similar bone burial rituals like that of the Jang Tapa. But it still remains a mystery as to why Winter Solstice was so significant both for the megalithic and the non megalithic folks that various ceremonies as that of the Jang Topa, Sankranti, maghe parob, and other observances were conducted on and from this day. Perhaps it had something to do with the sun's journey to its farthest point during the Winter Solstice when the sun was believed to have died and attained rebirth the subsequent day. The burying of the dead and the bones was perhaps congruent with such a belief. This idea associated with the sun may have persuaded the ancients to celebrate their New Year on the Winter Solstice day which subsequently got pushed back to the Vernal Equinox.

Let us now look profoundly into the Maghe Parob of the Hansdaya Mundari folks who celebrate the occasion around the Winter Solstice in late December.

For three consecutive nights subsequent to the sun set, the village boys would travel to the eastern boundary of the village beating their drums. From there they would turn towards the left and later they would return towards the eastern point in an anti clockwise manner[4]. This activity of the travel and return of the villagers is probably their symbolical enacting of the sun's journey from the equinoctial 'east' to the farthest point of the solstice and its subsequent return. But strangely, the sun's journey towards the left boundary does not imply to the winter solstice but the summer solstice. Now if this exercise of the Mundas is the figurative description of the sun's course which according to my belief it surely is, then why do they duplicate the sun's journey of the summer solstice phase during the winter solstice?

Another inexplicable feature of this ceremony is their crooning of Haua songs during the night of the Mage Parob. During their performance the leader would lead the song and the group would soon fill in with shouts of "Haua", "Haua". Van Exim thinks that such songs are meant for the nature gods also known as the Bongas.

The boys invite him to the festival and the songs gradually get vulgar and obscene. Van Exim rightly believes that Haua songs indicate a 'fertility rite'. It is difficult to conjecture the definition of Haua, but Julian Cope refers to Robert Graves in "The Greek Myths" as Hawwa or Haua to be the Mother of all living 'things'; who too is a fertility Goddesses.

Hindus have created very complex and varied ranges of calendar today combining the much primitive observational astronomy, Vedanga jyotsiha and the much later developed Siddhantas or theories of astronomy. Developing a calendar not only requires the deep understanding of the paths of the celestial bodies, profound knowledge of the sky and even erudition in mathematical calculation based on time and movements of the planetary bodies. The adivasis may have had a calendar at some earlier period but that doesn't seem to be much in vogue today. For the Hindus their new months begin with the full moon much in contrary to that of the tribals whose new month commences with the new moon[5]. Sadly, these people have a complete lack of script therefore if ever they may have had a calendar it must have been oral. (The so called Harappan script found on seals has been researched to have been found to be the Santali script[6] which however has not found wide acceptance).

A question comes to mind that if somewhere in the past the tribals did have an understanding of astronomy for which they may have raised the megaliths for observation of the celestial bodies then why is there a severe lack of it today? This of course I have tried to crack in a later chapter.

The practice of raising megaliths as a memorial or burial in accordance to mathematics and astronomy was widespread all over the primordial world at a time when the glory of the Great Mother was sweeping every where. But why so much of hard work, astronomy, geometry and intelligence were put to use for the erection of a primitive megalith? The answer as discussed in a previous chapter perhaps lay in the fertility of the land. Various rituals and ceremonies of the fertility cult brought down from much primeval times confirm that they perhaps believed that sunrays on the earth on different days of the year amplified or lessened the productivity of earth. World over, these days of the escalation of fertility of the Great Earth Mother were needed to be celebrated therefore the sunrises and sets were required to be viewed through the megalithic observatories to identify the precise days.

Few major alignments of Punkri Burwadih and Birbir

Alignments are things which need to be seen to be enjoyed. Today however we cannot say for certain why they created such views by way of orientations and alignments. But then watching these creations today we can surely appreciate this civilization's primitive folks' deep understanding of the landscape and their relationship with their megaliths. Every primitive megalith had various forms of alignments; let me discuss a few of these from two of my most favourite megaliths, Birbir and Punkri Burwadih.

The long stone and the small triangle in Birbir always puzzled me why they were there. One fine day realisation dawned in me and I saw that the positioning of the two stones was done with a purpose as they were actually placed simultaneously aligned to the two hills of Kesura and Silwar in the horizon parallel to each other (Pl.60). Observing more intensely I found that the small triangle was made to replicate the triangular Kesura hill in the distance (Pl.61) (Please look at the *photograph* for a better understanding).

A constant frustration lingered in me as to why the menhirs in the Punkri Burwadih megaliths have been placed in that manner...what could have been the possible reason? There must be a certain alignment which I was unable to grasp...and then I saw it. Facing the North West of the monument I discovered that the three menhirs were in reality positioned to mirror the peaks of the Tandwa hills in the horizon (Pl.59) (Please refer to the *photograph* for a better understanding).

These two alignments are remarkable paradigms of outstanding engineering of the primitives which facilitated such dramatic sights and better still that these engineered views can still be thoroughly enjoyed.

References

1. Subhashis Das. Sacred Stones in Indian Civilization. Kaveri Books
2. Surendra Prasad Sinha: . Life and Times of Bhagwan Birsa. Tribal Research Institute.
3. Van Exim. The Religious System of the Mundas. Catholic Press.
4. Ibid.
5. Van Exim. The Religious System of the Mundas. Catholic Press.
6. N.K.Sharma. Echoes of the Indus.

12 More Astronomy and Mathematics

Mainstream archaeologists in India do not relate megaliths with astronomy and mathematics or anything else other than death. The iron slags found littered all around the megaliths confirming the onetime presence of the iron smelting Asurs do not interest them either. It is a pity that orthodox archaeologists fail to look beyond accepted norms of things; refusing to see things not in their books! When I had taken an archaeologist of the Jharkhand State Archaeology Dept to show him the lizard/tortoise hybrid dolmen of Banadag (Pl.53) he was unable to comprehend the primitive monument commenting 'he had not been taught about this', therefore he does not know such structures hence this cannot be a megalith.

This was a ridiculous and a laughable retort from a responsible officer of the State Government who pronounced that in order to 'see' unknown things; he is required to be taught! Even a child without a trained eye can spot the lizard. Col Dalton was neither a trained archaeologist nor a qualified anthropologist yet his tireless field work was just more than perfect. Had his research and finds not been documented, much of India's enigmatic past would have remained untold. He cites such animal monuments as "...if set up in honour of deceased friend or hero, is credibly carved into representation of some animal." In regards to such fusion of animals in to megaliths he writes, "It looks like a cross between a camel-leopard and a horse. It is I believe, the Bir Sadom of the Kols, the jungle horse, the Nilgai, Antelope picta"[1] The primary interest in megaliths for archaeologists is what lies beneath them and their surface architectures are of not much value for them. Their measurements, inclines, orientations and alignments all being representational signs are hardly a matter of significance for them.

Megaliths in India, I believe can be primarily divided in to four types, the first being the burial and memorial kind housing urn or pot burials, cist circles containing sarcophaguses *et al* many of which can be dated back to over 2000 BCE. Tribals are also known to raise menhirs commemorating major events to have been accomplished in their village or in their commune. Erecting stones to demarcate the boundary of their villages was another function of megaliths across the ancient world. The astronomical type of megaliths comprising burials is another category of megaliths which has been ceased to be made today. Countless small pot burials may even be found in such tombs. Such megaliths could serve as observatories and calendars also. The final variety is the non-sepulchral chaste astronomical type meant to perform precisely for astronomical reasons. These have no correlation with death whatsoever therefore no burials have been unearthed from them. Despite the disparities in their purpose these monuments were worshipped and revered as temples as megaliths were the first temples ever created by the prehistoric humankind[2]. Many of which are still worshipped and such rituals in these stones have been instrumental in saving many of these archaic monuments from complete obliteration.

Let us now explore a few of such megaliths in India which are not connected with sepulchral uses. In Asota in the North of Pakistan, there is an enigmatic but a significant megalith (Pl.11). This shrine has neither revealed any burial nor relics of any kind been recovered from here. Originally comprising of 32 tall stones, scholars have yet not been able to conceive the purpose of this stone circle[3]. Modern research has also shown to the scholars that the Asota megalithic complex was in reality a sun temple of the sun-worshipping communities in Saravish regime ($5^{th}/6^{th}$ cent BCE)[4]. Scholars are of the view that every stone pertained to each day[5]. Even the Burzahom megaliths in neighbouring Kashmir in India have not revealed any burials hence the purpose of these megaliths is still not known either[6]. The megaliths of Maski in Karnataka excavated by Thapar in 1957 have also not revealed any sepulchral association[7].

Therefore, the belief that all megaliths are only graves or memorials of the dead is erroneous. In my earlier book, I had articulated that not all megaliths were sepulchral but many were observatories too somewhat like the megaliths of Hanamsagar, Vibhuthihalli (Karnataka), Nilurallu (A.P), Punkree Burwadih, Jagannath pahari and Manjhadiha (Jharkhand). Therefore, it's not surprising that archaeologists who have always held megaliths as burials as they have been taught to think likewise are not able to recognize the objective of these megaliths of Asota and Buzahom as these prehistoric monuments were erected with the purpose of observing the course of the sun and other celestial bodies.

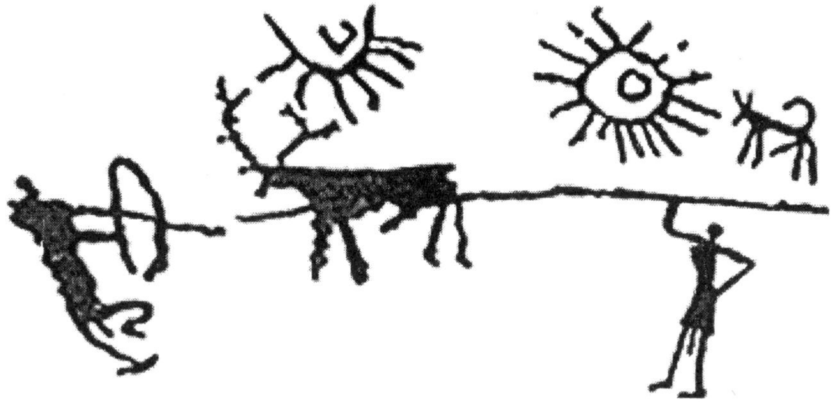

Fig.6

This is a Neolithic art done on a rock near the megaliths of Burzahom. There are two suns depicted in the scene for which there are no plausible explanations. May be the artist was depicting some celestial phenomenon.

Carlleyle believed that the stone circles of Deosa reveal such intricate measurements which were perhaps built by someone who "...can understand the significance of such measurements in a Druidical or Magian sense". He also believed that "...the aboriginal fort of Tontpur was full of significant measurements...."[8]. Allchin too had found many megaliths in South India which were not connected with death. He indicated that orientations towards sunrises might have been in use in such non sepulchral megalithic architectures[9]. Among the foreign authors too there are many who believe that not all megaliths were solely raised for funerary purposes but even for scientific purposes and even for worship[10].

The practice of burying the bones of the dead in small urns next to the menhirs in megalithic complexes is persistent till date. Such a custom in rural Jharkhand, Bihar and MP is known as sat-bharwan. In many places this custom is even called satgarhwa or satgarha. Megaliths have always been believed by the early villagers as stones which are 'alive' as the rural folks tend to believe that these stones grow towards the heavens above. Perhaps this correlation of megaliths with the sky where God resides had the villagers bury the bones of their deceased in urns next to such stones hoping facilitation of a proper birth in the next life[11].

Let us now probe into the word Satgarha or Satgarhwa which the non tribals have been using for megalithic burials from very ancient times.

Md. Hameed, a Lecturer from Panjab University of Lahore mentions in his paper on a mausoleum in a place called Satgarha in Pakistan lands up with various explanations for the name[12]. They range from a 'neat house' to 'true house' (in Sanskrit) to one even from Cunnigham who interprets the name as 'seven castle or forts'. If only these scholars would have been aware of the proto austroloid Mundari tribals, their languages which once was prevalent from Afghanistan to the Mekong valley and their migratory lores in which they claim to have entered India through the region where this Satgarha in question is.

Satgraha as discussed above is a custom of burying bones still prevalent in places as Jharkhand etc. The term Satgraha has stemmed from the convergence of two terms 'Sat' meaning 'bones' (origin unknown, could be austric the non- tribal peasants and the tribals in Jharkhand do not use the term 'sat' broadly for all bones but for the ones meant for burying) and 'garha' is a burial of these bones (of the deceased). The name must have been ordained by the locals for burials (second burials, after the cremation) of the Mundaric tribals which were perhaps built years before even the mausoleums in Satgarwa in Pakistan got made. These burials which provided the name to the village may have been built thousands of years from today during the Mundas' stay in here. Many names in present Pakistan is surprisingly Mundaric; confirmation of their stay in here thousands of years ago. We will further deal with this phenomenon in a forthcoming chapter.

Disappearance of Tribal Astronomy

A question frequently crops in my mind where had all the profound mathematics with which the older megaliths were once laid, disappeared? Furthermore there is also an understanding that megalithism is an uninterrupted tradition in many parts of India, then why and how could the ancient skill disappear? If the archaic astronomical megaliths be ascribed to the ancient Mundas, Asurs, Hos or the Oraons then why do they not reveal any memory of such understanding?

Profound pondering has me to mull over two practicable clarifications; first of all it could be that the designers or the architects of these inextricable sites and their builders may have been two different sets of people. The megalithic Mundas, Hos, Oraons or the Asurs were perhaps the ones having no knowledge of astronomy or mathematics but were proficient in hewing and positioning megaliths according to the precise measurements regimented to them by the astronomer priests. The astronomer-priests were perhaps the architects of the astronomical megaliths who may have been the brains behind these sites possessing all the knowledge on these subjects. The Magis/Sakaldweepis could have been the only scholarly lot in those days holding so much of wisdom within them.

Being well versed in astronomy, astrology, mathematics and medicine the Sakaldweepis or the Magis were perhaps the most erudite lot during hoary times. How they had flourished into to such a knowledgeable set of people at a period when the rest of the populace lingered in obscurity of superstition and blind beliefs is something very difficult to resolve.

In India, the Sakaldweepis today are spread all over the country and they claim themselves to be the descendents of the primitive Magis and argue that they were brought here from Sumeria by Shambo, the son of Krishna. Magis were also the people believed to be responsible for the prediction of Jesus' birth who prophesized by gazing at a star in the night sky; a symbolical gesticulation of their wisdom in astronomy. Legend has it that they were also the people who had constructed the solar observational temple of Konark[13].

Although there is a prevalent belief which suggests that the Sakaldweepis and the megalithic Sakas are the same set of people, yet there are no scientific evidences what so ever to prove that the Sakas and the Sakaldweepis were the same lot. The Sakas were a near savage, power hungry warring people who were driven out by the Yu-Chis from Central Asia; their original homeland. They attacked India and set their empire in Malwa Kathiawar, and parts of Maharashtra. Their kings called themselves Satraps and later they Hinduised themselves but are known to speak in their own languages and wrote in Greek characters on their coins.

The confusion has risen due to the closeness of the names of Sakas and the Sakaldweepi. The Sakaldweepi Magis on contrary to the barbaric historical Sakas were not a war loving but a scholarly community who did not rule but spent their time in scholarly activities. They were well conversant in Sanskrit, did not write in Greek letters, and subsequently became the priests of the kings where the conventional Brahmins refused to go. Soon they were elevated to the status of Brahmins for their erudition. Therefore, the belief that the Sakas were the Sakaldweepis is an incorrect perception which can easily be eschewed. Both the Magis and the tribals share quite a few likenesses, as both inhabited the same region of Sumeria / Chaldea. Both the communities had forts called purs which were believed to have been placed at straight lines quite similar to the alignments of the primitive megaliths.

If the Magis had really originated in the region of Sumeria as they affirm to be, we should not forget that the tribal Kolarian Hors too had their origin more or less in the same region. These two communities must have been acquainted with each other in Sumeria. Both the tribals and the Magis may have had accompanied together into

India or their entries into India might have occurred at different stages but were united again in India at some later period.

The Magis, according to Bhavishya Purana were brought to India to construct a sun temple at the region of Multan in the western part of India at the 'sunset' or 'asthachala' phase, for the sun's 'mid-day' or 'madhayachala' phase a sun temple was built by the Magis in Mathura. Eventually to study the sun during its 'rise' or the 'udayachala' stage the Magis were assumed to have set up a temple at Konark[14]. Whether there was another original temple created by the archaic mythical Magi astronomers on whom the present day famed sun temple of Konark today stands, is difficult to say. There could be a remote possibility that the Sakaldweepi Mags being sun worshippers and observers of its transits may have had built a few megaliths too with astronomical affinity as that of Punkree Burwadih and even on a few places where Hindu temples were built in the later periods. The megalithic Mundas, Oraons, Baigas, Asurs, Gadabas and Sabars etc being efficient stone cutters may have been employed by the Magis in the construction of these megalithic temples.

The Santals too place their homes in alignment to the headman Majhi's house in the village. Such an alignment is known as 'Pantai'. It also may be that the Magis were accompanying the tribals wherever they drifted to as perhaps the Magis had become some sort of head of the megalithic tribals who had helped the Magis build many megaliths of scientific significance. Although no tribal legends confirm such a presumption but isn't this strange that the headmen of the Santals are also known as Majhi, a word so near to Magi.

In years to come both the megalithic Kolarian Hors and the astronomer priests; the Magis parted ways to such aloofness that does not deem probable today that they may had been together once to build numerous astronomical megalithic observatories. The tribals bereft of the knowledge of the sciences during their days with the Magis still remains the same.

There could be another likely explanation for the phenomenon of the tribes not demonstrating their knowledge with which the astronomical megaliths were built in the past. Some event could have occurred in the ancient times which may have had been instrumental in expunging the knowledge of astronomy and mathematics among the tribals. The undisclosed explanation probably could be assigned to the prevailing religious and social conditions of India. The primordial astronomer-priests of the tribals may have been very well-informed of these sciences by inheritance and by observation of the transits of the celestial bodies with which they once raised the megalithic observatories.

The onset of Vedic Brahmanism, the rise of Buddhism, Jainism and Ajivika sect and their swift burgeoning across the wide expanse of India in due course of time had many tribals relinquish their religion and convert to these newer faiths. The term Munda could be ascribed to the shaven heads of the Buddhist Bhiksus (*Mund in the Hindi signifies a bald head*); identifying a person with his physical condition or disability is a very old practice.

During this period of a few centuries when the tribals had embraced the new religions, their former animism and their trivia of horizontal astronomy and mathematics in megaliths were gradually erased from their remembrance. By the period of Ashoka, Buddhism had the entire nation under its sway; Jainism was spreading to a few pockets of Orissa, Jharkhand, Bihar, Bengal, Karnataka, Tamil Nadu, Rajasthan, and Gujarat.

The emergence of the Guptas saw the resurgence of Vedic Hinduism and the gradual downfall of both Buddhism and Jainism. Although the Guptas were tolerant towards both these religions and patronized them, nonetheless the revivification of Brahmanism transpired during them. The resurrection of the Brahmin religion and the advent of Shankaracharya witnessed the decline of Jainism, Buddhism and megalithism in India and people began reverting to their former Hinduism. This was the phase when even the tribals too were slipping back to their old ways of tribalism discarding their adopted Jainism and Buddhism Chokahatu is quite a large tribal village adjacent to the megalithic site which houses quite a sizeable Jaina population;, nearly half of the village and the rest of them are tribals. These tribal Jainas are know as Sadak jainas who worship Parashnatha. This substantiates the theory that these people were converted to Jainism from tribalism but when Jainism ended here few as these Sadak Jainas may have had retained their ancient Jainism mixed up their form of animism.

Megalithism too was gradually revived but the primitive wisdom of astronomy, mathematics and other sciences that the tribals were once in possession of and with which they had once raised such momentous ancient monuments, were long forgotten without practice. Graham Hancock rightly comments, "We are people with amnesia..."

The convention of bequeathing megalithic burials and memorials for the selected few died away. Practically every tribal in a village began receiving megaliths after their death, like as today.

Chokahatu and Alignments

A tribal generally builds a megalithic burial or memorial in the same burial site which was laid thousands/hundreds of years ago aligned to hills and astronomical orientations. Say for instance, the Chokahatu megalithic burial of the Mundas, one of the largest megalithic sites in the country spread over a whopping 8-acre of land and comprising of over eight thousand burial slabs[15] (Pl.41).

During my visit to Chokahatu, I tried finding the reasons why the primitives were invigorated to uphold the site to such a momentous eminence that the site would hold so many burials and continue to be used till date, since over two thousand years. The answer I found lay on the alignments; the burial site had been unerringly positioned between Burunda and Hesadih hills which are exactly on the North-South directions from the megaliths; a rare phenomenon indeed. As north south is the position of the laying the dead, Chokahatu therefore was a natural choice for the Mundas to be made a burial with the two hills on its North South. It was this event which made Chokahatu so significant that its glory spread to far flung places and people still flock here to obtain a stone slab for their departed.

The megalithic graves in the present day tribal villages of Jharkhand are also known with names, as sasandiri, haragrahi, jangarhi (*I have found even in Gujarat many stone circles are called Jangarha*) etc and most of them are very old which have been positioned according to primitive alignments. Even the newer graves, dolmens or menhirs are positioned inside the old haragrahis or harsalis which are already aligned. However many modern day memorial menhirs have been found to be placed at random devoid of any alignment or astronomy.

The very primitive mathematical stone models of Bodhayana Shila (which I named after the pioneer mathematician of 6th cent BC) and Vishwa Shila in the Jagannath Pahari of Hazaribagh with megaliths of Rola, Punkree Burwadih, Hanamsagar etc are evidences of complex mathematics once prevalent among the primitives when this enigmatic civilization may have reached its phase of eventual flowering. How could the tribals have possibly built such models of mathematics without any script? They surely must have been acquainted with numerals lacking which they could have done the lengths, degrees, ratios in the megalithic complexes.

Calendars

A very primitive bone discovered from near Lake Edward on the border of Zaire and Uganda later named as the Ishango Bone was found to comprise a series of similar small parallel notches. These indentations on the relic are believed to represent the lunar calendar apart from being the oldest table for prime numbers. The horn in the right hand of the Venus of Laussel found at the opening of the cave of Dordogne, assumed to have been sculpted around 25,000 BCE has thirteen small cut marks which too are considered to be the thirteen months of the calendar of the moon. Similar thirteen (month) notches has been reported from all around the world.

In the prehistoric Jabra Road megalithic site near my hometown of Hazaribagh, one fine morning I had stumbled upon a stone elephant. Elephants are sacred animals that are still icons of fertility. Images or small statues of elephants are still a prerequisite in Hindu marriages of many communities. Adjacent to it on the flat stone surface I discovered a small set of parallel lines in an east-west direction (Pl.65). Eleven lines were unmistakably perceptible, but two more faded lines could also be spotted. If these two lines were once a part of the remaining parallel lines here, then these would total up to a series of thirteen lines which may have been etched in the shadowy past to correspond to the thirteen month lunar calendar.

In rural India, the women folk apply small vertical parallel striped lines of red vermillion on sacred stones with their fingers. The Santhals regard such small vertical lines as their various deities as Marang Buru, Lita and as other Eras etc. Be it natural altars, wells or megaliths as of the menhir of Lohsingna; such small vertical lines consecrates the object on whose surface they have been drawn, hence the mark themselves too are revered as sacred (Pl.46). Could it be that these small parallel vermillion strokes which are deemed auspicious were actually counting signs or numerals of the ancient period like the parallel etches on the various bodies as described above?

On many horizontal stones in several megalithic complexes two rows of eight cupules with sixteen cavities in each can be found. Today village children can be seen playing by placing small pebbles in the cavities. It could that these patterns of cupules found of horizontal stone were actually lunar calendars. The pebbles used by the village children today may have had origins in the primitive modus operandi of placing such stones in these cavities for counting the lunar days. The sixteen cupmarks could pertain to the 16 day waxing moon.

Nevertheless such cupules are different from the other form of cupmarks which are without a definite pattern and can be seen profusely marked on a stone and are normally associated with the ubiquitous Mother Goddess.

Henges turned into ponds

In my former book I had put forth this hypothesis that old ponds which have raised sides and are circular in shape in reality are very ancient megalithic henges which in due course of time got transformed into ponds. In many rural districts I observed that like megaliths these 'ponds' too were created in exact alignment to hills

(Pl.64). My speculation was thus confirmed that the science of alignments was also applied in the positioning of these tanks as they were placed on the Gita Lines between two hills and/or in the intersection of hills on its either sides; principles also employed in the positioning of the prehistoric megaliths. With the advent of Brahminisation of the country, the ancient cult of megalithism came to an end. Consequently veneration of these structures too became increasingly defunct. Like the megaliths, the henges too fell to disuse and gradually rainwater filled them up transforming them into ponds. Henges in India got completely forgotten from human memory as now these henges serve a different purpose as ponds.

Many scholars in UK believed that similar henges were dug out for the purpose of an observatory of the rising stars[16]. Chris Knight and Robert Lomas believed that such artificial ditches were made as mock horizons which enabled the study of the rising stars[17].

Observations of the stars from the ditches were also done with the rims of the ponds working as artificial horizons[18]. Archaeologists in Britain believed that many of such henges were filled with water to function as a "reflector disk"[19]. Hence if several megalithic architectures are identical and were raised for the same purpose both in Britain and India then henges too in both the nations may have had been created for the similar principles.

I would like to mention here one particular ritual done in the concluding day of the Durga Puja which I feel has connection with the observation of the stars on the waters of the henges. In the morning of the *Dashami* or the tenth and the ultimate day of the Durga Puja a circular utensil filled with water is placed near the feet of the idol of the Goddess. Devotees view the deity's feet on the water of the circular container locating the correct angle else the sight could be missed. The circular water body could be a distant memory of the circular henge filled with water and the act of observing the idol's feet could be reminiscence of the observation of a certain star on the water during these days prior to the Hinduisation of the custom and its later enjoinment in the Durga Puja.

References

1. Col.E.T.Dalton. Rude Stone Monuments in Chutia Nagpur and other places. Thorsons.

1. Julian Cope. The Modern Antiqurarian.

2. www.geocities.com/zulfiquar155history.html

3. Ibid

4. D.H.Gordon. The Prehistoric Background of Indian culture. Munshiram Manoharlal Publishers.

5. Ibid.

6. D.K.Thapar. A.K.Sharma. Indian Megaliths in Asian context. National Museum Institute.

7. D.H.Gordon. The Prehistoric Background of Indian culture. Munshiram Manoharlal Publishers.

8. Allchin, F.R., 1956. The stone alignments of southern Hyderabad. Munshiram Manoharlal Publishers.

9. Terence Meaden. The Secret of the Solstice. "....they have been called burial chambers or mortuary circles - mistakenly seen as abodes of the dead instead temples for the living." Souvenir.

10. Subhashis Das. Sacred Stones in Indian Civilization. Kaveri Books.

11. Mohammad Hameed. Mir Chakar Khan Rind and his mausoleum at Satgarha: An obscure chapter in the History of the Baloch in Pakistan. Putattatva 39. 2009.

12. Kalkut. Shambo

13. Ibid.

14. Ibid.

15. E.T. Dalton. Rude Stone monuments in Chutia Nagpur and other places.

16. John North. Stonehenge: Neolithic man and the cosmos. Harper Collins.

17. Chris Knight and Robert Lomas .Uriel's machine. Fairwinds Press.

18. Ibid.

19. Ibid.

13 Punkree Burwadih Date Decoded

The positioning of megaliths on a precise location depended on many aspects, the Sathpatha Brahmin states that burials must be made on a flat, desolate and infertile earth slanted towards the north where there should a be a river with its water flowing from South East[1]. The Brahmin further states that these burials should always be exposed to the sun and should be accessible for worship[2]. My study shows that they did not arbitrarily select the spot for their planting of the megaliths but much went into account prior to the selection of the spot. Hills were a prerequisite for the building of the monuments as they were aligned to them.

The Cross in a Circle mode was employed while erecting a megalith which was acquired by connecting them to the hills in the circular horizon by way of the alignments. The idea behind it all was perhaps to create an omphalos by connectiing the hills by way of alignments and at the meeting point would the megaliths be positioned. Hills were regarded very consecrated by the early denizens and still are by the present day tribals, we have no confirmed explanation for the ancients' alignment to hills. Such intersectional points created by the alignments of hills were hold very sacrosanct even substantiated by the Vishnu Purana which dubs such meeting points as sandhi sthals on which sacred puras were built. Gandharvas, Rakshasas, Yakshas, Daityas and Danavas reside here, it states. Such holy were these locations that they were deemed as heaven on earth by the Vishnu Purana where no sinners can tread even in their hundred lives.[3]

Kosambi also noticed this phenomenon who cites that the primitive savages had placed their Mother temples at the junction of roads[4].

I have found that apart from such Cross in a Circle (which allows hex sectioning too) single linear alignments have been applied for the erection of megaliths. Being inadvertently on such alignments had facilitated trees, stones obtain hallowed status in the past which they enjoy even today[5].

Although a megalithic complex may have been placed in keeping with such alignments, the stones within it have been found to be oriented towards major sunrises or sets or towards cardinal points. I have found that the calendrical or observatory type megaliths as that of Punkree Burwadih (Pl.67), Napo, Nillurallu have been sited on raised lands (this may or may not be man made) to assist easy sunrise and set viewings.

Tony Crerar, as stated in one of the early chapters believes that the primitives were in look out of the alignments of Rola as *"they (the primitive astronomers) undoubtedly recognised the significance of your latitude for allowing hex-sectioning of the circle...and possibly, if they came from elsewhere, had predicted this situation and calculated where to find it by long experience from establishment of other alignments in territories to the north or south of you"*. He further believed that "*The trained astronomer would immediately recognise the potential of the Rola plain ringed by mountains when walking into it on a clear day and indeed, might have been actively searching for it"*.

This is ridiculous; I would say to myself, what on earth Tony was stating, 'latitudes'? Were these people really aware of coordinates of the earth? Much surprises waited for me when I learnt the coordinate of the Punkree Burwadih megaliths; it was 23 deg 52' 20".

N. Kameshara Rao, the former professor of Indian Institute of Astrophysics, Bengaluru emailed me quoting that Punkree Burwadih was surprisingly in close proximity to the Tropic of Cancer whose latitude is 23 deg 26' 16" N. One of my geographer friends calculated to find out that the Tropic of Cancer missed Punkree Burwadih by approximately 50 kms. 50 kilometers seemed too far to be offered a tick on the idea that the megaliths were really intended to be placed on the Tropic of Cancer.

Later, studies revealed to me that the Tropic of Cancer does have the feature to change at a very leisurely pace of approximately 46.8 arcs second per century. Rao Sahab calculated the change and found that 23 deg 52' 20" WAS the coordinate of the Tropic of Cancer on about 1518 BC!

This therefore would mean that the megalithic complex of Punkree Burwadih must have been made on this year i.e. on or in close proximity of 1518 BC when the Tropic of Cancer had passed over this particular location! Punkree Burwadih is aesthetically created on a raised piece of land with each stone made to align to main peaks and notches of the encircling hills and also towards the cardinal points and with the Tropic of Cancer passing over it there could have been no better place than this for raising such a megalithic observatory.

They surely were searching for this spot as Tony had suggested. The primitives must have waited for the Tropic of Cancer to arrive at this spot and subsequently they must have created the site on that year. But did they really understand Tropics and Equator?

How else could they have positioned the entire megaliths on this latitude if they were not aware of the co-ordinates? Simple, Rao explicated that the megalithic people might not have known the concept of Tropic of Cancer but would have noticed that the sun would have been exactly over their heads at noon on one specific day when vertical stones and humans cast no shadows on the ground; this was the mid summer sunrise day or when the sun shines on the Tropic of Cancer. The following day they may have had observed that the shadows were beginning to elongate.

(Apart from the sunrises of the equinoxes and a few other significant mornings I have found that on the summer Solstice mornings one can observe the sunrise through the "V" of the menhirs in here.)

This date of 1500 BC also perfectly matches with my hypothesis of the proto austroloid Kolarian tribals' arrival into the region in their migratory process in to Jharkhand from the Biblical lands.

References

1. 13.8.1.4 Satpatha Brahman
2. 13.8.1.13 Satpatha Brahman
3. 2nd ansh. 2nd chapter 46-49. Vishnu Purana. Gupta Press.
4. D.D.Kosambi : Myth and Reality. Popular Prakashan.
5. Subhashis Das. Sacred Stones in Indian Civilization. Kaveri Books.

The Book of the Hors

1 ORIGIN

Tribals. Also known as, the adivasis were perhaps the first known entrants into India prior to the arrival of the Dravidians and the Aryans. History offers no mention of tribal contributions in our evolution as a nation as if they contributed nothing significant in the progress of India; India behaves in such a manner as if they did not exist at all.

Once a major force of India, the adivasis today are a disillusioned lot, losing every bit of their self-confidence and respect; they have either succumbed to Christianity, Islam or has adopted the Hinduised way of life, chaste tribals unaffected by the major religions are a very few. Many still linger in acute hunger and neglect, the government is trying to do everything possible for them. Communist Naxalites have exploited them to their core in the name of their upliftment.

The adivasi culture is different, of which the average Indian remains completely ignorant of. The bulk of the country's population either regard them as Hindus or Christians. Either of the beliefs is flawed, like their culture the tribal's religion too is different, which the average Indian doesn't care to know. However the formation of newer tribal states of Chhattisgarh and Jharkhand has certainly given an impetus to the tribal cause. In tribal Jharkhand their religion has now got a new name; *Sarna dharm,* with origins in their sacred grove '*sarna*' thereby ousting the infamous British conferred 'animistic' and 'others' in the religion columns of Governmental documents. Many tribal festivals and ceremonies dormant till now have surfaced once again.

Ancient Brahminical texts have not been considerate towards these early inhabitants of our country. The common man without knowing much about these people spills disdainful and contemptuous annotations on these less fortunate early inhabitants of the country. That they were a predominant population in the country once is unknown to many. Rai Bahadur Sarat Chandra Roy, the doyen of Indian anthropology rightly states, "......not even a chapter of decent length is allotted to these people in any standard work of history..." and also "...India should have been named Kolvrata"[1] looking at the large numbers of Kolarians living in the country, once.

Quite rightly like the modern day history books, the ancient Brahmanical texts, the Jaina Puranas, the Tripatakas have not voiced kind words for these ill-fated citizens of this sacred land. It is as if these people never existed for the so called civilised India. A community as old as theirs, witness and even participants to so many events of history of the world cannot be possibly devoid of their own history. True they are folks bereft of any script therefore were incapable in recording all the accounts of their lifetime. But all these are admirably logged in their folklores; a very primitive and time-tested documenting tool; many a times more authentic than books.

The Puranas tend to be differing with each other on various episodes but there are diminutive differences in the tradition of these adivasis. Sung during significant occasions and passed on to the forthcoming generations by their elders these traditional stories are no less than oral history, and they have a lot to say but is anybody listening? Ask them. They are over enthusiastic to narrate the stories of their origin, of their traversing in the Middle East in the very ancient times, of their journey into various countries including India, to all.

Let us look in to their migration narrative; it is significant in many ways; as it informs us these people's ancient history despite the fact that there aren't many archaeological testimonies to confirm the validity of these tales. The proto Austroloid Santals, Mundas, Hos, Asurs and even the Dravidian speaking Oraons recount much similar folktales which suggest that they are not indigenous to this land as usually regarded to be but these tribes had entered India from outside the nation earlier than the Aryans.

Despite the minor disparities, their fable of origin and their migration narrative remains much similar. Nearly all the Santal Gurus and the scholars agree that their origin was somewhere in a place called Hihri Pipri. It is however difficult to trace this ancient mythical city along with other towns, water bodies and hills today, as named in their tradition. Nonetheless there is a belief by and large among the Santals that their origin was somewhere in Sumeria. This opinion was even nurtured by D.B. Kisku[2] along with many other Santali scholars. Rev L.O.Skerfudd too cites in the Santal Pargana gazetteer that the Santals had once occupied Persia.

The Kolarian tribals believe that prior to their entering into India either they had dwelled in Sumeria/Chaldea which they believe was their place of origin. These tribals call themselves Horko, Hour, Hor or Ho, splitting up the term 'Hor' or 'Hour' it is apparent that the term/s must have stemmed from the confluence of two words 'Ho' and 'Ur'. While 'Ho' is the archaic idiom for 'people', 'Ur' was the tutelary Goddess of the ancient capital city of Chaldea located to the south of Sumeria. Ur lent her name to the city which was supposedly the original native land of these people. 'Hur' or 'Hour' would therefore simply imply to as being 'people of Ur' or 'people who revered the Goddess Ur'[3].

Origin of terms such as Herr or Aryan which are words to address people can be traced to the much ancient tribal term of 'Ho' or 'Hor'. In rural Bihar, UP and Jharkhand 'Ho' is abundantly used to beckon both men and women. 'Ho', I have been told is also used in Africa to address female folks. 'Hey' has been used in various ancient Sanskrit literatures to invoke both the male and the female. Even in the English language, 'hey' is a major term for a call. The English word "Horde" may be tracked down to the word 'Ho', which according to the Oxford dictionary means 'a large group of people'. The Collins dictionary however is more explicit in elucidating the term "horde", according to it 'horde' is "a troop of nomads" stating more rightly the wandering lifestyle of the ancient Kolarian 'Hors'.

Another assumption that these tribes had originated from Chaldea lies hidden in their being called 'Kol'. Koldea sounds so similar to Chaldea if only the 'Ch' is pronounced as a 'K'. The Rig Veda conveys that the inhabitants of Chaldea were once known as 'Kaldis'[4] probably because they once were the residents of 'Kaldea' or 'Chaldea', therefore they were called Kols. There are many names of towns and villages in India with the name of Koldiha which sounds very near to Chaldea or Koldea which merely means 'the Diha of the Kol tribals' or 'the habitation of the Kols'[5]. It is quite possible that the Koldihas /Koldeas in India are named in the honour of their earlier homeland of Chaldea.

In North India there is a profusion of names of villages and cities having prefixes of 'Kol' as Kolchea, Kalchi, Koldiha, Kolihan, Kolghatti particularly on the purported migratory route of the tribals into mainland India. The name of the city of Kolkata can also be associated with the word 'Kol'. These all suggest that these places were once occupied by the erstwhile Koalrian tribes.

Gudea, one of the kings of Chaldea who is known to have founded the city of Laggosh had also founded a kingdom and a clan or a killi by his name. The Kolarian Khadias in Jharkhand still retain Gudea as their titles which being their clan or killi hints at the supposition that their origin could be traced back to the Gudea of Chaldea.

References

1. S.C.Roy. Mundas and their Country. Crown Publications.
2. D.B.Kisku. The Santals and their Ancestors. Career Press.
3. Subhashis Das. Sacred Stones in Indian Civilization
4. R.K.Choudhary. Prachin Bharat ka Rajnitik ebam Sanskritic itihas. Bharati Bhawan.
5. Subhashis Das. Sacred Stones in Indian Civilization. Kaveri Books.

2 In the Land of the Bible

Kolarian legends talk of their peregrination in the region of the Central Asia and the Middle East for a very long period in their dim past[1]. The Santali gurus and scholars believe that many names of towns, seas and hills in their tradition can be traced to these regions. This is more than mere coincidence that quite a few tribal myths can be found documented in the Old Testament. These also confirm that the Asurs, Santals, Hos, Khadias, Mundas and other proto austroloid Kolarian adivasis were once living in these lands of the Bible.

The forthcoming pages citing many affinities between the Old Testament and tribal India will attempt in establishing the hypothesis that the Horites must have travelled to India in the remote past. If this be true then it would be that both the contemporary Hors of India and the Horites of the Bible must be the same set of people.

Genesis describes a group of people called Horites, Hivites, or Hurrians although scholars today differentiate Hurrians from the Horites. The traditions of the Khadias, Asurs, Mundas, Oraons and the Santals etc assert that they once lived in these lands of the Bible in the remote past. They, as informed earlier were and are still called Horko, Hor or Hour which are surprisingly close to the Biblical Horites.

The study of many names of villages, hills and rivers in India reveal the lesser known fact that they are austric in origin. These names which have strangely been retained since hoary antiquity surprisingly finds mention even in the Old Testament. The only logical clarification for this phenomenon could be that in antiquity while entering India from the Biblical land the Kolarioan Hors must have been naming their villages, rivers and mountains on their migratory path in memory of the names of their former villages, rivers and hills in the land in and around Central Asia.

It is generally accepted that these Horites of the Genesis had origins in a region identified as Cimmeria somewhere in the Caucasus Mountains. However, many hold Cimmeria as a fabled land of imagination. Ptolemy presumed that the Horites of Genesis had their origins in Cimmeria. Surprisingly, the Santal Hors talk of a land called "Cim" or 'Sim Disom" in their migratory legends which they had once inhabited in much ancient times and which might be corroborated with the legendary land of Cimmeria or Simeria which in short may be labelled "Cim" or "Sim".

Curiously, many villages named "Cimmeria", "Simeria", and "Simariya" or even 'Simra" can be found on this migratory track of the Kolarian Hors into India (Pl.4). 'Cimmeria', 'Simeria' or 'Simariya' are surely the same name with dissimilar spellings. The adivasis must have named these villages in India in remembrance of their abode in the so called fabled land of Cimmeria in the remote past. For the tribals, 'Cim' or 'Sim disom' is a very significant city or region in their tradition whose glory they often sing during their ceremonies.

The king of Gomorrah according to the Old Testament was a Horite called Birsha. Birsha incidentally is a very popular Kolarian Hor tribal name across India. Birsa Munda is also the name of the celebrated tribal born in Jharkhand and is venerated as a divine person. In Genesis, Birsha's city is Gomorrah which Ptolemy assumed to be of Cimmerian origin. In North India, many towns and villages comprise the same name of Gomorrah or with marginal variants as Gomrah, Ghormarah, Garumarah and Goma etc. The presence of so many Gomorrahs in India is another substantiation that the Hors must have named these villages during their exodus into India in memory of this significant town in the Biblical lands where they must have been residing once.

In Genesis, we learn that the Horites lived in the land south of Cannan. It also mentions a town called Seir and further states that the original inhabitants of Edom trace their ancestry to Seir (Gen 36/20-21). The name of the town owes to a person of the same name, Seir who incidentally was also a Horite (Gen 36/20-21). The Santals narrate the story of one Hor called Ser (Seir) Singh who had driven all the Kolarian Hors away from Seir Disom. Ser or Seer Disom in their tradition is an ancestral city named perhaps after the villainous Seir(2). Genesis affirms that the descendent of Seir was Lotan who too was a Horite (Gen 36/20-21)!

Lotan surprisingly is also a very popular adivasi name of the Kolarian Hors even today. Apart from the above, the names such as Tamar, Jibeon, Jabal, Keenan, Mitkah etc found in the Bible are still maintained by the modern day tribal Hors in India as name/s of their villages, hills, ponds and rivers.

Santals steadfastly believe that Abraham was infact their forefather as they consider the term of Abraham to have been emerged from the convergence of two Austric words of "Abba" (standing for father) and "Haram" (denoting an old revered person)[3].

It is a surprise that quite a few stories of the Bible and those of the Santali folklores are very similar to one another; the devastation of the cities both in the Old Testament and that in the Santal myths are reasonably identical. The only variation in the story is that in Genesis God demolishes four cities of Gomorrah, Sodom, Admah and Zeboiim where as in the Santali folklores Thakur Ji (one of their highest ranking gods) destroys only one town of Khojquaman. Startlingly, even the reason for the destruction of the towns in both the stories is quite alike: mounting immoral sexual conduct of its denizens.

'Sodom', another Horite city also possesses an Austric Mundaric denotation called 'a horse'. Naming villages, clans and people after animals, birds, flowers and trees was a common practice in the ancient times which the Kolarian Hor adivasis still maintain. The king of Zeboiim, a city which God had destroyed, was Shember, who too was a Horite. Shember too is a very popular tribal Hor name in India since very primitive times. Shember also finds mention in the Rig-Veda as the great anarya (non Aryan) king whose hundred forts were not only plundered by the archetypal Aryan god Indra but was also eventually exterminated by him, therefore The Rg-Veda pronounces Indra as the Purandar or the demolisher of (non Aryan) forts. The rishis untiringly sing the praises of Indra in the Rg Veda for this 'magnanimous deed' of killing the 'Asura'(non Aryan) Shember.

Shamber is also a river adjoining the Caspian Sea, a few European cities have names as Shember or even Shemberg; all these perhaps in honour of the archaic Shamber.

Talking of a few more similarities between the Bible and the tribal traditions is the similarity between the terms Zohar/Zoar and Johar. If the first one is a Biblical city for which God shows mercy sparing its from destruction the later is an austic term employed by the tribals in India for greeting one another. "Johar" is also a term which the Serbs pronounce during a toast. I kind of feel that there seems to be a liaison between God's prevention of Zohar's obliteration as mentioned in the Genesis and the using of a near similar term, Johar as salutations by so many people ranging from Serbia to the tribal Hors of Indian heartland.

What follow consequently of the event of the obliteration of the cities as conveyed in Genesis is that Abraham and his daughters seek refuge in the caves of a hill. The Santali version of the same story subsequent to the demolition of their city is that the sole survivors were a young man and a woman who sought refuge in Mount Harata. Here they had stayed for quite a long time till their numbers swelled.

Santali scholars equate Mount Harata with Mount Ararat[4]. However, in The Old Testament there is a mention of one Mt.Hor in the region. Is it probable that the mountain was thus named as because the Hors or the Horites may have had taken protection on that hill to escape the holocaust? In Hebrew speech Horite means a group of people living in caves. The folktales do articulate the tribals had taken shelter in the caves of a hill, now the obvious question which comes to mind is whether these people were named Horites for the fact they were residing in caves of this hill after Khojkaman's ruination? Surprisingly Egypt had a Pharaoh by the name of Hor in the 13th Dynasty at around 1760 BC. Whether he was connected in any way to our Hors or Horites in question will make a very interesting piece of research.

The Mundas celebrate a festival (parob) called 'Ed' or "Ind Parob"; a name very close to the place Edom, this definitely advocates a connexion between the tribal 'Ed' and the Biblical 'Edom'.

Modern Archaeologists segregate Cimmeria in to two wings; the western group of the Thracian Sumerian and the eastern faction of the Kizil- Koba - Colchins. In North Bihar and Nepal, there resides a set of austric tribals called Tharus or Tharos. Tharus are supposed to have arrived here in the past from Rajasthan[5]. However there is no way of knowing of their race from their face as today they are more close to the relatively fair skinned, depressed-nosed Nepalese folks rather than the dark skinned adivasis. Despite it, anthropologically they belong to the proto austroloid group and they speak the austric language and could possibly be a sister wing of the Santals, meaning that they too are an offshoot of the archaic Horites and may have roots in Cimmeria. Their name Tharu/Tharo appears be concomitant with the western Thracian wing of the Cimmerians who subsequent to the entrance into India went on to be called Tharos. The Santals, Mundas, Khadia, the Hos, and other Kolarian Hors or the Horites on the other hand could be correlated to the eastern group of the Kolchins.

References

1. D.B. Kisku. Santals and their ancestors. Career Press.
2. Umashanker Santalo ki kahani.
3. Subhashis Das. Sacred Stones in Indian Civilization. Kaveri Books.
4. D.B.Kisku. Santals and their ancestors. Career Press.
5. Sulagna Chattopadhya. The Tharu of Don. G n Y. Vol 8. Mar-Apr 2008.

3 The Affinities, Yet Again

There are many hazards in locating the migratory routes of the dark complexioned adivasi Hors into India with the likely assistance of their legends. Many of the narratives articulated by the tribal Gurus are as old as the hills therefore variations have quite naturally seeped into them.

Here in this chapter we would hunt for the common affinities between India and Europe/UK which confirm to the incredible human connexion between these far placed lands during the remote past. Terence Meaden asserts 'Neolithic India bore similarities with Neolithic Britain and Ireland'[1]. That there was a connexion between UK and India was realized by many scholars even in the British era as Keshab Chandra Sen, a foremost Brahma Samaji scholar of 19th cent Bengal stated... 'in the advent of the English nation in India we see a reunion of parted cousins, the descendents of two different families of the ancient Aryan race..."[2]. Scholars like Sen saw this similarity from the Aryan perspective as because the Dravidian and tribal perception was unknown to them.

The conspicuous affinities between UK and India is perhaps the outcome of a connexion in hoary times between these countries, occurred due to the possible migration of the proto austroloid Mundari Kolarian Hors to Europe and their consecutive arrival into India. These Kols must have carried their glory and reverence of Goddess Ur and other fertility goddesses with numerous other influences with them to Europe and must have brought the rituals of the denizens of these lands into India. The disparities among the sequence of the placement of the towns in the narratives vary from one tribal Guru to other. As for instance, Guru Budhan Kisku[3] states that the Santals were in Kapsara prior to Sasan Beda and places their stay in Khojquaman much at the end of their journey into India somewhere perhaps in Afghanistan.

Umashanker and D.B.Kisku however places Khojquaman prior to their stay in Sasan Beda. Both Umashanker and Guru.B.Kisku sets the Santals' refuge in Mt. Harata following their stay in Hihiri Pipri. Umashanker maintains that their shelter in Mt Harata was twofold; initially after their retreat from Hihri Pipri and secondly, subsequent to the destruction of the city of Khojquaman by Sin Bonga or Thakur Ji. D.B. Kisku seconds Umashanker in the tale of the Santals' refuge in the caves of Mt.Harata after Thakur Ji wrecked Khojquaman thereafter too both agree that in the city they had indulged in promiscuity. Despite their differences in the viewpoint of these scholars, the names of their ancestral cities, woods, and lakes precisely remain the same. If variants and contradictions of the same events are conspicuous in different Puranas, then oral tradition too can have the liberty to differ from one another.

The Khadias state that their original homeland was in a place called Hirapur.

Hirapur jonme thanro ampah
Hirapur bhuihar thanro ampah[4]

Translated into English:

Hirapur is your place of birth
Hirapur is your place of origin of your descendents

The Munda legends also speak of a migration which is different from those of the Santali. Their oral migratory chronicle in their early nomadic days reports their traversing in the following cities consecutively starting at Ajobgarh, thereafter to Kalinjargarh, Garh Chitri, Garh Nagwar, Garh Delawar, Bijnagarh, Garh Pali, Garh Piprah, Mandar Pahr, Nandan garh, Rijgarh, Ruidasgarh and thereafter into Jharkhand[5].

In order to set up a proper scientific sequence of the Mundas' trek, scholars normally peek into India. The names in the Munda folklores have been equated with the cities in North India. Significant scholars like S.C.Roy, M.G.Banerjee and even Kisku believed that the Azobgarh of the Munda tradition is the present day Ajamgarh in U.P. I am a little sceptic about the original Ajobgarh, it is just not that simple as it seems to be. Ajobgarh to my understanding doesn't seem to be in India, I place the Mundas' initial homeland of Ajobgarh somewhere near ancient Cimmeria which as discussed earlier is also supposed to be the home of the Horites. That the water mass in close proximity to the Caucasus Mountains, where Cimmeria must have been, is called "Sea of Azov" confirms that the Mundaric "Azobgarh" must have been in the vicinity of this sea.

Although the rest of the cities of Mudaric traditions cannot be tracked and identified today but there are evidence still left in and around the Sea of Azov to substantiate the presence of the Kolarian Mundas here in the remote antiquity. Towns and villages around the Caspian Sea and Sea of Azob still bear names which are Santali/Mundaric. That these names which have survived the ravages of time are of a tribal origin are known to none as the bulk of the Hors had departed from this region thousands of years ago. Names like Kumdag, Nabitdag, Jandag and Kopetdag around the Caspian Sea are undoubtedly Mundaric/Santali similar to many tribal village names in Jharkhand as Katkamdag, Banadag and Jordag etc. Therefore the presence of austric name in the region in Central Asia confirms that these Hors must have once resided there many centuries ago.

From Turkey to Afghanistan there is an abundance of ancient Austric names as Kurrah, Qura, Kasmar, Kunar etc for towns, villages, rivers and mountains etc. which have still been maintained in present day India for the same objects as above. All these must have been nicknamed by them during their stay in these areas in the remote past in their onward journey to India or else what could be the possible explanation for the identical names?

One more aspect in the entire migration episode is that tribes like the sedantric Birhors and Juangs do not reveal any migratory tradition. The Oraons, Khadias, and Santalis firmly consider that most of the towns refered to in their tradition are outside India and they had migrated into this land like the Aryans in the remote past. Their other common belief is that their land of origin is Sumeria (Chaldea) and that they were the authors of the Indus Valley Civilization.These Kolarian Hors' traditions affirm that they had spread into many parts of the world from Sumeria/Chaldea and their languages and cultures had influenced the ancient world which is apparent till date[6]. The Santali folklores in a way speak of such a spread all over; but being a sedantric, unassuming and a docile lot without a script, their history was undocumented in texts hence remaining unnoticed. The Santalis talk recount one Jarpi Desh in their migratory traditions which many scholars as Kisku correlate with Europe judging with the closeness of the pronunciation of the words. Apart from this there are also a few leads which authenticate these nomadic people's one time presence here in the distant past.

Family names like Kole, Cole, and Kohl etc predominantly among the Germans could be a distant memory of the presence of the original Kols in this land in the hoary past who may have contributed to these people's surnames. D.B.Kisku quotes 'The Encyclopaedia Mundarica"[7] authored by the late erudite Father J.Hoffman has some startling facts about these Kols. The late Father had long researched and had found similarities of Mundaric and many European words. Below is a brief list of such words:

MUNDARI	EUROPEON	MEANING
ASI	ASK (English)	to ask
BURU	BURG, BERG (German)	mountain
KUI	KUH, COW (German & English)	calf
DA	DA (Latin)	to give
DURANG	DUANG (Irish)	song
GOLAD	GULPEN, GULP (Flem, Eng)	to swallow
HAKE	HAKEN, HAAK (Flem)	to hang
HI or HIJU	HIK, HIC, HERE (Ger, Lat and Eng)	to come
LADI	LADEN (Ger)	to load
MA	MAAIEN, MAHEN, MOW (Flem, Ger, Eng)	to cut
MEN	MEAN, MEENEN, MEINEN (Eng, Flem, Ger)	to mean
NE	NUN, NOW, NU (Ger, Eng, Flem)	now
NARE	NAH, NEAR, NADER (Ger, Eng, Flem)	near
HOR	FIR, VIR, WER (Gaelic, Latin, Old English)	man
ABRA	ABRI (prevalent in England, origin: unknown)	natural holes, caves or rock shelters.
BULU	BIL (Flem)	thigh
AIUM	AIO (Greek)	to hear
OR	OR (Greek)	to drag
PAHAL	PFLUG, PLOEG, PLOUGH (Germ, Flem, Eng)	ploughshare

The above list shows a few of the many Munadric present in many European languages which is certainly indicative of the Santals' and the Mundas' presence in the region during ancient times. The similar typology of megaliths both in India and in distant Europe is certainly another testimony of contact between the adivasi Kols and the primitive British.

Sasanbeda is one of their ancestral places in the Santal tradition where the Santali Hors had once resided. Naively the tribals mix up 'sasan' with turmeric as it too literally means the same. Many scholars consider Sasanbeda as 'a land of turmeric' and many have even linked it with the 'Yellow River' in China. But only a handful knows that in Jharkhand a megalith is called 'sasandiri' or just 'sasan'. It is weird that in remote Germany, megaliths too are dubbed as 'sazzen', a term very near to Kolarian 'sasan'. 'Saxum' is a Latin word also close to 'sasan' which also implies to a big rock. In distant UK megaliths are either sarsen or sasan which surprisingly is the term in Jharkhand for megaliths! The stunning similarity in the names for megaliths between Jharkhand and Europe is definitely amazing, but is a solid confirmation of this presumption that the dark skinned Kolarian Hors must have travelled to Europe and UK and must have therafter journeyed back to India with their megalithism.

Reverting to Sasanbeda it seems the term is the upshot of the union of two words 'sasan' and 'beda' ; 'sasan' implies to megaliths and 'beda' in the Mundari languages means 'fence'; Once translated into English, Sasanbeda means "a fence (or a circle) of megaliths"!

In UK; there are numerous stone circles as that of Stonehenge, Avebury and Callanish which do resemble a fence of megaliths. Is 'Sasanbeda' of the Santal folklores in reality a 'megalithic fence' and does it indicate their stay near such megaliths in the UK in the remote past? The Santals are not megalithic today but they could have been such in the past but their sister community, the Mundas are still megalithic raising megaliths after death. A legend popular about the megaliths of Callanish is that a high priest had accompanied a few black people who arrived here on a boat from beyond the seas and had constructed the Callanish megaliths[8].

Gradually archaeological testimonies of migrations to long distances are surfacing. Recent disclosures have suggested that a 14-year boy has been found buried in the premises of Stonehenge[9] and[10]. The interesting part of this story is that this boy had travelled to Stonehenge from a warmer climate possibly from the region of the Mediterranean Sea. The skeleton has been dated to about 1550 BCE. Prof Jane Evans believes that 'visitors were travelling to Britain specifically to see Stonehenge'. The boy must have journeyed in a group "to Britain from Spain, Italy, Greece, or France, crossing the English Channel in a primitive wooden boat". The find of the skeleton of the teenager also known as the "boy with the amber necklace" confirms that migrations did take place to Britain from South Europe in antiquity (Bronze age in this case). Mike Pitts, editor of British Archaeology states that despite the fact that archaeologists are fighting the idea of migration during this period, "there were individuals moving across huge distances." Dr Andrew Fitzpatrick, of Wessex Archaeology believes that "people had been travelling great distances for thousands of years for trade and exploration."[11]

Even Thapar and Sharma believes that the striking similarities between the megaliths in Asia 'points out towards a cultural link in the distant past"[12]. However, these influences could have been a both sided affair too. Chances are also that the Santals could also have been carrying many customs and even words which had been loaned from the primitive Europeans and the British. 'Sasan' for megaliths might be a word which the tribals may have taken from the ancient British and was brought into India and Jharkhand during their onward journey to India.

The foremost evidences of possible connections between distant cultures other than archaeological vestiges and other similarities described earlier are the affinities of several rituals and religious customs. Even a larger proof of such a possible connexion in the past is when the same object bears an identical or a near similar name. As in the case of the term 'sasan' it stands for megaliths in Jharkhand and even in far-off England! In Keltic, 'bru' denotes a womb or a pregnant belly and 'brugh' is a tumulus. Quite similarly 'buru' in the Mundari languages is a hill which is also symbolical of the mother's womb or her pregnant belly. The term 'Abri' in old English means rock shelter or cave dwellings[13] and in the Santali languages, 'Abra' stands for a natural hole or a cave.

If in primitive Europe Ur and Ver were the primordial fertility goddesses, then Urvar or Urwer in India means fertility and in many places are still worshipped for the same reason. Even in primitive England there was a prevalence of the worship of Goddess Tara who is still worshiped in India[14]. Tara was infact a primitive non Aryan deity, absorbed later into the Buddhist and the Hindu folds respectively. Goddess Diya or the earthen lamp was also worshipped as the vulva of the Goddess in early UK much similar to that in India 'diya' is also the symbol of the Goddess's womb[15].

Apart from the Kole and Cole or Kohl syndrome described earlier, Germany has a city called Weimar. Incidentally there are many villages by the name of Baimar, Bahimar in India which sounds so close to Weimar which denotes that both Weimar and Baimar are undoubtedly the same names with a marginal variant. The Mundas and the other proto austroloid Kolarian Hors worship in the sacred grove which they term as the Sarna.

In Europe and in America there are many towns and villages whose names are close to 'Sarna', as 'Sarnen' in Switzerland and 'Sarnia' in North America and in many parts of the world confirm the presence of these Kolarian Hors in these parts of the globe. One town in Sweden is solely named 'Sarna'[16]. The Kols' influence on the European languages and culture is visible not only from many similar words as shown in the above but even from many celebrations and customs in Europe and UK.

Celebration of the Equinoxes and the Solstices

These kols also have a very ancient ceremony called the Ba festival or the Baha parob (festival) which they equate with the Sarhul. Many tribals believe that Baha stands for flowers hence Sarhul and the Ba festival for them are same. Although both the ceremonies are connected today but earlier they must have been celebrated separately. In my last book, 'Scared stones in Indian Civilization' I had tried to disprove this present claim of the Kolarian Horkos that both the Baha festival and Sarhul festivals are the same. Research has revealed to me that Baha has roots in 'Visu' or 'Visua', the other name for equinox (more specifically, the vernal equinox) which occurs on 20th/21st Mar. Equinox in Sanskrit and the ancient languages are called "Vishuv" which today is known as 'Bihu' in Assam, Baha in Jharkhand, 'Visu' among the Malayalees, 'Visua" among the Sakaldwẹepi Brahmins[17].

According to the Hindu calendars the Winter Solstice called Makar Sankranti is celebrated on 14th Jan; an approximate push of about 21 days from the original midwinter sunrise of 22/23rd December. The Spring Equinox known also as Mahavishuv in Hindu calendars too has received a similar shove tentatively of 21 days to 15th April from the original Vernal Equinox day of 20/21st March. Communities like the Bengalis, Assamese, and Punjabis celebrate their New Year or on near the Mahvishuv day of 14/15 April with much singing and dancing. The Vernal Equinox in the ancient worlds too was commemorated with similar fun, dance and drinking.

Baha according to this theory is the sun; symbolised with a [yellow] flower. The observation of the sun it seems was prevalent in many megaliths where stones can be seen to be placed in alignment to the rising sun on specific mornings as the Equinoxes and the Solstices. Megaliths as Punkree Burwadih, Kesura, Jagannath Pahari, Manjhladiha, Vihuthihalli and Hanamsagar have features created by positioning of stones in straight lines to aforementioned sunrises. This custom being of tribal origin finds no mention in the ancient Indian texts (tribals, their lifestyles, sciences, religions barely existed for the ancient Brahmanical authors) but is retained in a few of the folk songs of the adivasis describing the observance of the sun through megaliths, among which one is described below[18]:

Amdore, sugare soben burum lelakada
Aguleme sasan Ba (Baha)
Sugare, horotanum, jangitanam,
Okopn Ba (Baha) pura sugare?

The song translates as, "O, you parrot you have seen all the mountains, bring me the yellow (?) flower. O you parrot you guard and protect them all, which flower is the best?"

Note the term 'Sasan ba' in the song which the translator applies to as a (yellow) flower or the sun.

The placement of the terms 'sasan' and 'ba' adjacent to each other here is interesting. 'Sasan ba' can be interpreted as a yellow flower, 'sasan' being a homonym means both a megalith and turmeric. The deployment of the term 'ba' or a flower symbolical of the sun adjacent to sasan makes it quite feasible that the poet here poetically refers to the event of viewing the yellow flowered sun through megaliths. Though now defunct, this tradition of viewing the sun through megaliths is still retained among the assorted rituals, folksongs and in the megaliths which wait for us to unravel their mysteries. Celebration of the Equinox is still convened by the natives around the Niluralllu megaliths in Andhra Pradesh.[19]

Study on the Punkree Burwadih megaliths has revealed that apart from being a burial it is also an observatory to study the transits of the sun constructed to perform as a calendar for the people far and near the megaliths. The Punkree Burwadih megalith for reasons like these must have been a highly venerated place.

Every community in India has their own calendar which is known in different names to different communities. None of the auspicious functions from naming of children, marriages, beginning of farming and undertaking important journeys to conducting the rituals of death etc would be held in India without referring to these old calendars or panchangs published every year. These calendars have origin in the post Vedic period are being designed by the Brahmnanical astronomers by combining both the Vedanga and the Sidhanta jyotishes.

But prior to the advent of the Brahmincal astronomer/mathematicians in India the tribal astronomer-priests learned of the dates through observational/horizon astronomy; monitoring the sun's varied position, Equinoctial and Solstical sunrises and sunrises of other significant dates. The dates were also confirmed by the certain position of the stars and the moon in the night time. All these were prior to the erudition of mathematical calculation. The previous chapter dealt how from the ancient times people learnt that on/from specific dates the earth's fertility is augmented or diminished. Therefore stones were set up with astronomical and mathematical precision so that the sunrises on these dates could be viewed with much exactness to procure the necessary dates.

Calendrical Intervals

To have such megalithic observatories function fairly accurately according to the requirements of the custodian priests of these monuments, it was necessary that each stone be positioned aesthetically and many a time with mathematical accuracy in alignment to major features of the surrounding hills and to major sunrises, sets, moonrises or sets or even rise of a particular star.

Antony Roper Crerar, the noted megalithic arcaheoastronomner from Wales had visited the sites of Rola and Punkree Burwadih with me and discovered stones alignments towards the Lunar Solstices.

Punkree Burwadih holds in herself many mysteries of the primordial astronomers. To unravel these unwritten secrets of science with which this enigmatic megalith was created had taken me years. Let me share with you a few of the unravelled sciences.

A small North-South aligned stone, marked as A is placed at a specific place from whose either edges one can see the sunrises through the "V" feature created from the positioning of the M1 and M2 marked menhirs on 15th Feb,26th/27th Oct and 26th/27th Feb , 15th/16th Oct respectively.

More candidly speaking, standing at the left flank of 'A' one can view the sunrises of 15th Feb and 26th/27th Oct. (Pl.66), while from its right edge of this very stone one can see the sunrise through the menhirs on 26th/27th Feb & 15th/16th Oct through the same "V" of the two menhirs.

The stone A therefore confirms that it has been cut to such an accurate size and thereafter positioned with such precision that the two edges of the either sides of this stone act as pointers for the sunrises of the above stated dates.

The megalithic calendar in UK considered a fiction by many, is approved by a certain sect of scholars. Antony, furnished me with the following megalithic calendar:

GREGORIAN CALENDAR	MEGALITHIC CALENDAR (Calendrical Interval)
21st Jun	CI 5 (Solstice)
1 Jun & 11 Jul	CI 4 & 6
6/7 May & 6 Aug	CIs 3 & 7 (midpoints)
25th Apr & 17/18 Aug	CIs 2.5. & 7.5
13th Apr & 29/30 Aug	CIs 2 & 8
2nd Apr & 10/11Sep	CIs 1.5. & 8.5
20th /21st Mar & 22nd /23rd Sep	CIs 1 & 9 (Equinoxes)
10th Mar & 3rd Oct	CIs 9.5 & 16.5
26th/27th Feb & 15th/16th Oct	CIs 10 & 16
15 Feb & 26th /27th oct	CIs 10.5. & 15.5
4th Feb & 7th Nov	CIs 11 & 15 (mid points)
10th/11thJan & 1st Dec	CIs 12 & 14
21st/22nd Dec	CI 13 (Winter Solstice)

The surprise here is not only how such an extraordinary wisdom of mathematics and astronomy could be obtained by the so called barbaric tribals in the deep antiquity, but also that the sunrise dates revealed by the stone A in the Punkree Burwadih megaliths correspond to the Calendrical Dates (CIs) of numbers 10.5 & 15.5 and 10 & 16 respectively of the megalithic calendar in remote UK.

The event proves that the stone A has been cut in accordance to the sunrises of the Megalithic calendar which in a way confirms the validity of such a calendar. The sunrises also demonstrate the same deployment of the same concept in megalith building architecture of Jharkhand and UK which thereby confirms a definite contact between the two far-away lands of India and England at some deep antiquity.

Commoness in Megalithic Architectures

Two years prior to his demise D.B.Kisku, the erudite Santali scholar and author of about seven books on the subject disclosed to me his various opinions and theories in his home in Dumka in the Santal Parganas, of which a few etched quite an impression in me.

The first of his deep rooted beliefs was that the Santals had migrated from Sumeria/Chaldea in to India and also that they had once worshipped the archaic

Goddess Ur in the ancient times and at long last he stressed that they had brought their Manjhi Thans (one of their open air temples) from their original homeland in Middle East . His belief might not have had any scientific foundation but that it emerged from his subterranean self where he was a diehard Santal, to me was of enormous accuracy.

Kisku's conjecture apropos the Majhi Thans was unknowingly seconded by one George Anderson, a professor of Old Testament from Edinburgh University. He claimed that the Canaanites who were later were known as the Phoenicians were much similar to the Horites in many ways. He cites that their altars had a wooden pole in its middle which was called Asherah (20). Surprisingly this in many ways bear resemblance to the Majhi. Thans of the Santali Hors (Pl.3) which too has a raised rectangular platform with a tall wooden pole of a Sal (shorea robusta) tree in the middle. The reason for the similarity is quite understandable as the Canaanites were the neighbours of the Horites in Biblical times.

If Asherah was the fertility Goddess in the Bible, a similar fertility rite called the Asherah or Ashariah Puja is still conducted by many communities including the Kolarian tribal Hors in East India during the monsoon month of Asharh in June-July to enhance the land's fecundity. The similarity of the name and the function could indicate that it must have been the same Goddess whose glory was brought in by the immigrant tribes in to India from the Land of the Bible in the much ancient times.

Speaking of a few other similarities between UK and India, we find the reverence of particular shaped hills known as the pregnant Recumbent Mother Goddess form (Pl.51); a contrivance of the obsolete primitive fertility religions which were widespread from ancient America to England to India. The mode in which the pregnant Recumbent Mother Goddess form of the Amjhori hill is framed in Punkree Burwadih (Pl.69) in Jharkhand can also be seen in UK done to the hills in the landscape with many megaliths.

Consider another likeness between primitive Britain and India can be tracked to Terence Meaden[21] who has made some spectacular and brave discoveries of human heads carved on many megaliths ranging from Stonehenge to that of Avebury.

The book substantiated my belief that the megalithic Kolarian Hors did really have a communication with Britain in the remote past. Why do I speak this, is because somewhere in the mid nineties I too had the fortune of discovering two heads in Jabra and one colossal sized one near the famed Hathia Pathaar structure at the banks of the Damodar River in Phusro. They looked so impossible to me, I was kind scared to reveal them to the world. Eventually Meaden's book enthused in me the nerve to feature the head of Jabra Road in my former book. Later on I learnt of another megalithic head in Kakrabhat, Chattisgarh[22].

Once, I was surveying a ruined megalithic site of Banhe which I had discovered a just few weeks back, when I spotted a small pale stone sticking out from the wall of a dig next to the megaliths. I pulled the stone out along with a few tools and potsherds and carried them home. I washed them under the faucet and subsequently studied the tools and the potsherds but for some unknown reasons I kept the small sandstone aside for some other day and then I forgot about it.

The first thing in the morning I did was to fish out the small stone from amidst my numerous collections of various rocks and stones. Adjusting the stone to the inflowing light, what emerged in front of me was perhaps one of the greatest surprises of my life. The small 4 × 2½ cm sandstone piece revealed about two animal heads, couple of human profiles, a possible turtle head and even a headless nude Mother Goddess (Pl.50)! The subtleness of the artistry was superb revealing the artist's delicate understanding of the stone that had used its undulations and even a small ingrained pebble as features of the various profiles and an eye respectively.

What purpose did this relic serve, I have no idea but this could be understood that the sculpture must have been very significant for its curator.

Wonder whose heads were these?

Did the human heads belong to the dead ancestors of the custodian or were these of some unknown deities?

Judging by the tiny headless Mother Goddess with her pregnant belly with a deep navel and prominent breasts (Pl.50) though eroded with time confirmed that this should be a relic of the very primitive fertility cult.

Therefore the find of heads in all sizes from Avebury in UK to Kakrabhat, Phusro to Jabra in India and not to forget the tiny riddle relic with multiple heads from the vicinity of Banhe megaliths authenticates the worshipping of heads during the prehistoric megalithic era must have been a common phenomenon across the world . Small stone figurines of reptiles, animals and even phalluses have been found from the states of Jharkhand and even Orissa[23]. The function of these figurines must have been what the riddle stone was to these early inhabitants of the country.

References

1. Terence Meaden. Stonehenge The Secret of the Solstice. Souvenir.

2. Romila Thapar. The Past and the Prejudice. NBT.
3. Guru Budhan Kisku. Jomsom Binti "Kherwal Hoponkoak Sirjom kahni". The Asiatic Society.
4. W.B.Archer. Khadia Song Book.
5 Mundas and their Country. S.C.Roy. Crown Publication.
6. Subhashis Das. Sacred Stones in Indian Civilization. Kaveri Books.
7. D.B.Kisku. Santals and their Ancestors. Career Press.
8. Julian Cope. The Modern Antiquarian. Thorsons.
9. www.bbc.co.uk
10. www.dailymail.co.uk
11. Ibid.
12. B.K.Thapar and A.K.Sharma. Indian megaliths in Asian Context. National Museum Institute.
13. Julian Cope. The Modern Antiquarian. Thorsons.
14. Terence Meaden. Stonehenge. The Secret of the Solstice. Souvenir.
15. Ibid
16. Subhashis Das. Sacred Stones in Indian Civilization. Kaveri Books.
17. Subhashis Das. Sacred Stones in Indian Civilization.
18. D.B.Kisku. Santals and their Ancestors. Career Press.
19 N.Kameshara Rao, Puja Thakur, Yogesh. Megaliths of Nilurallu www.megalithindia.in
20. Christopher Lomas and Robert Knight. Uriel's Machine. Fairwind Press.
21. Terence Meaden. The Secrets of the Avebury Stones. Souvenir.
22. B.K.Thapar & A.K.Sharma. Indian Megaliths in Asian Context. National Museum Institute.
23. R.N.Bhattacharya. Pre-historic Stone Figurines in Eastern India. Journal of the Asiatic Society. Vol XLV 2003.

4 THE JOURNEY INTO INDIA

Beginning from the East of present day Iran or West Afghanistan and Pakistan to states of Bihar, Jharkhand and Bengal in the East of India one can come across many villages having names prefixed or suffixed with particularly two words of 'kalan'/ 'kala' and 'khurd'. In other words, there would be two villages of identical names placed in propinquity, of which one name may be suffixed with a 'kala' and the other one with 'khurd'. Even Kabul, the capital city of Afghanistan has its 'kalan' and khurd versions. The capital city is a 'kalan' where as Khurd Kabul is a few kilometres South East of the capital city of 'kalan' Kabul. This 'khurd' 'kalan' phenomenon which begins from the west and shows an eastwards trend confirms the movement of the 'khurd' 'kalan' people towards the east.

Their meaning and purpose of prefixing and suffixing to the village names is still not fully comprehended. One interpretation by the villagers themselves is that 'kala' or 'kalan' denotes a larger village where as 'khurd' stands for the smaller ones. There is another explanation which suggests that villages once had a tradition of moving from one spot to another hence the former situated village is believed to be called 'Kalan' and the later one as 'Khurd'. However 'Kalan' may have an astronomical penchant as kalan could also indicate to the various phases of the moon.

Tracing the source of both the words of 'Kalan' and 'Khurd' words is difficult, but if they have originated in the west then probability is that the word could be Prakrit, Pisachi, or Mundari etc. All these explanations of these two terms of unknown origin are merely assumptions; their real meanings still keep eluding us.

Suffixing of the term 'kot' to names of villages and towns as Diwankot, Pathankot tends to begin from the west of India or Pakistan and can be traced even to Jharkhand, Bihar and Bengal where villages can be seen having names as Mangalkot, Jalmankot etc. which again is evidence of people's movement from the West to the East.

The journey of the Kolarian Hors into India from Sumeria/Chaldea is well documented in their songs as those of the Santals. But judging by the typology of the megaliths we can very well understand the megalithic Mundas had entered India from the north crossing Peshawar, Mingora, the Swat valley and Kashmir. The presence of the sun temple of the megaliths of Asota and names of places as Mangora, Kharna (relates to the chaat parab of east India), Chakai, Tundi, Jhumra, Bhera, Bairat, Rohtas, Dehkal, Muree and many more which can also be found on the migratory routes in the West and North West of India of these tribes deep into the land or even in Jharkhand where eventually the majority of them settled.

Palash as a name of a town in the region of Swat valley amazes all as Palash is a major flowering tree of the tribals of Jharkhand. Kunar is a river in Hazaribag but to find it in Afghanistan region and that too as a river confirms that the Kols had also named the river in Hazaribag after the Kunar river which in Afghanistan on its banks they might have once lived prior to their entrance into mainland India[1].

Swati is a river in Pakistan which is also the name of a now dried up river near the megaliths of Banadag in Jharkhand. All these are proofs of the Kolarian Hors' journey into India from the west as they went on naming many villages with more or less the same names where they lived earlier in the Central and West Asia and Sumeria; a phenomenon that has been discussed in detail in a former chapter. The Kashmir region too holds names for towns as Kud, Rewali which are Kolarian in origin and are also found in the Mundaric region of Jharkhand confirms that this was the route taken by the Mundas while entering India from the Swat valley and Asota. The Burzahom megaliths in Kashmir too are confirmation of the megalithic complexes erected possibly by the erstwhile Mundas during their stay here.

Santal folklore tradition talk of a city of their ancestors called Jhaldak. My surprise knew no bounds when on the map I caught sight of a town named Jhaldak just over Kandahar in Afghanistan. The find of 'Jhaldak' confirms that it isn't a fabled city after all, it being there is solid evidence that the Santals were here thousands of year ago and also that the folklores of these tribals are true and their migration into India through this course too is also authentic.

Read the song below which my research compatriot the late D.B.Kisku had documented[2].

The one here is a song which the Santals sing describing a battle they had raged during their stay at Kandahar in Afghanistan.

Cete lagit mapakkana,koendako,
Dhao,dhao Kandaharire?
Cete lagit gopockana Badoliko
Dhao,dhao Kandaharire?
Sima lagit mapakkana Koendako
Dhao,dhao Kandaharire?
Onda lagit gopockana Badoliko
Dhao,dhao Kandaharire?

In plain English the above ancient Santali song translates into

Why are the Koendians put to sword?
Raging in Kandahar
Why care Badolians killed
With fierceness of battle in Kandahar?
For the border (land) are the Koendians put to the sword
Raging in Kandahar
For the pieces of land are the Badolians killed
With fierceness of battle in Kandahar?

The Santals, Oraons and even the Khadias claim that it was their predecessors who had authored the Indus Valley Civilization. Nirmal Verma had found many similarities between their Khonds and the so called Indus script on the seals[3]. These Kolarian Hors and even the Dravidian speaking Oraons sing lot many songs in memory of the Indus valley, Punjab and even Rajasthan. They even sing in remembrance of crossing a desert in the antiquity; 'Hahakar' is a term they normally identify a desert with[4]. 'Sinjho' nai is the Indus river; the following ancestral song of the Santals is one of the numerous songs which the late D.B.Kisku had amassed[5]. Songs as these are sung during most of their major occasions. The song mentions the 'Sinjho nai' or the Indus during their stay in here:

Kara kadae jobelena Sin'jo naire
Sin'jo naire na kurikin maha naire

The English translation to this song stands as below:

Blind buffalo wallowed in the river Indus (Sinjo naire)
In the river Indus, O, two girls
In the Great River.

However, it is somewhat hard to believe that it were only these austric tribals who were residing here; Indus valley civilization must have been cosmopolitan in nature. Hence it would be imbecile to assert that there was a preponderance of a single race and lingua franca in the region. There ought to have been many races here speaking various languages. Scholars as Emeneau, Burrow, Kuiper, Mayrhoifer, Witzel, Luboitsky and Parpola believed that people in the Indus region may have spoken a para Munda apart from Dravidian, an ancestral language of Burusashi, traces of languages of Bactria Margiana Archaeological Complex, Iranian and Indo Aryan of the North Western fringes (6). Even Southworth believed that austro Asiatic language as para Munda was perhaps popular in the region[7]. Like as the eminent linguist Suniti Chatterjee, Levi too strongly believed that Munda languages were a great influence in South Asia.

As discussed at length in a former, even today names of countless towns, villages, rivers or hills in India and Pakistan have been retained from the dark past are austric Mundari and not Sanskrit in origin. The phenomenon is the fallout of these tribals' stay in the region in the antiquity. The presence of a town by the names of 'Sental' in Punjab is also another confirmation of the presence of the Santals in this area at a very early period of time. There is a town called 'Bunga' on the eastern side of Indus which could be the mutilated form of the word 'Bonga' which is a spirit/god of the Kolarian Hors. Rohtas, Sandi, Tanda, Maholi, Kora, Kunda, Arararia, Gola are a few more names among thousands others which are of austric origin and can also be traced on the migratory track of the Kolarian Hor tribals in M.P, Chhattisgarh, U.P, Jharkhand, Bengal, Assam and even in Bangla Desh. Much of this migratory tract is strewn with megaliths which were perhaps raised by the various Mundari tribes during this journey. Few of these tribes settled in the lands and the rest walked ahead, perhaps as destined.

These tribal austric words wouldn't mean a thing to the present day Hindu and Muslim residents of these towns as no such primitive tribes reside there anymore. At times they are even found to interpret these names in their own perspectives but never even once would they know that these languages are of tribal adivasi origin as they once inhabited the region before migrating either to the South or the east of the country.

I had in my earlier book discussed how these tribes settled in areas as if specifically demarcated for them. Their lands were segregated by boundaries of forests and hills[8]. In Jharkhand the Santals settled in Hazaribag for a very long period. The Dhanua Bhanua woods in the North West and along with Rajauli, Parasnath, Lugu and

Chutupalu hills were made their boundaries. Centuries later the majority of them moved onto the land of Satbhum of Bengal. Much in the similar lines we find Mundas too having their own piece of land in Ranchi with boundaries marked by the Chutupalu, Bundu, and Chakradharpur hills. Similarly, the Oraons, Asurs and the Hos too live in such demarcated lands. However today Jharkhand has about 32 tribes, in the past this number must have been more. Many tribes have been assimilated in to some other or may have faded away with time. Tribes like the Savaras who were in much predominance in Jharkhand in the olden days are in quite minimum here today but are in good population in Orissa. The Mundas claim that it were they who arrived in this land first therefore they had been named Mundas or the head. For this, however they use the term 'Khuntkatti' to describe their claim on the land as they were the first arrivers in the region.

The Asurs, another Mundari tribe famous for being the first iron smelting tribe of the country whom many associate with the Hittites, shun the claim of the Mundas. They believe it were they who had arrived in the land first but were driven away by the Mundas[9]. The megalithic Asurs were believed to have fled to what we know today as Chhattisgarh carrying along with them their iron smelting technology and from there they wandered south. According to many Asur myths they were driven away by the Mundas[10]. The megalithic Mundas are believed to have followed them south as far as to Kerala. Here they confronted with more megalithic building tribes who may have sailed in through the sea route. However the Kolarian Hors travelled beyond the frontiers of Bihar, Bengal to the region of the North East. At Nartiang in Meghalaya the dolmens are so similar to those of the older Mundaric dolmens as found in Chokahatu in Jharkhand suggests the presence of the Mundaric tribes or their influence in dolmen making in the region in the past.

Returning to the so called 'allocated lands', one can spot such demarcated lands in nearly every state of India. The separation of the tribes is so neat and precise as if someone led the tribal Hors into this by allocating their lands. This land distribution reminds one of assigning of lands and primitive cities to various tribes by Moses, Joshua according to the wishes of God in The Old Testament.

References

1. Subhashis Das. Scared Stones in Indian Civilization. Kaveri Books.
2. D.B.Kisku. Santals and their ancestors. Career Press.
3. Nirmal Verma. Echoes of the Indus.
4. Swarnalata Prasad. Santhali Hindi Shabdakosh. Tribal Research Institute.

5. D.B.Kisku. Santals and their ancestors. Career Press.
6. Madhav M.Deshpande. Aryan origins: Brief History of Linguistic Arguments. India: Historical beginnings of the concept of Aryan.
7. Southworth Franklin. Linguistic Archaeology of South Asia. Ingram
8. Subhashis Das. Scared Stones in Indian Civilization.
9. Dr. Satya Prakash.The Asurs. TRI.
10. Van Troy. Developing the Prehistoric. TRI.

GAZETTEER

Subsequent to the Kolarian tribes' entry into India, they mounted to their pinnacle of their political, social, cultural and astronomical expression here as because they left behind stunning relics in stones discernible all over the sacred land of India confirming such a presumption. These relics in the form of megaliths, henges, mounds and stone sculptures are so varied and diverse that it is mind boggling. This civilization of these unfortunate primitives is not mentioned with much respect in our ancient sacred texts but with a great deal of disdain and abhorrence. Their Gods have been eschewed and their religion scoffed at. Their cities destroyed and their people exterminated at the inane most pretext. Ironically all these were documented by the Aryan Brahmin writers themselves in the Vedas, Puranas and other sacred texts.

The finds of large number of megaliths across the country confirm that India was a flourishing tribal land once prior to her Aryanisation. These relics in the form of megaliths and stone sculptures being tribal in origin are not acknowledged as source of history/prehistory of India despite the fact the country is literally interspersed with these primitive temples.

The following pages reveal a few of very ancient rock sculptures and megaliths discovered by me and others.

Let the mystery of these nameless structures stay and be food for imagination for all.

I love them that way.

1 (Bhandra) Lohardagga

Apart from good roads Lohardagga is also connected with Ranchi by a single train which plies between the two cities at convenient intervals. Bhandra is a block village about twenty kms on the Ranchi Lohardagga highway. Once in the village take the south road and reach the hill about a km away. There is a tribal village at its foot. Ascend the hill and at the north-eastern part of the hill you confront with a dumbfounding architecture; a right profile of a dog's head (Pl.17). This huge sculpture of the animal's head on stone is so life like that it not only astounds the viewer but makes his heart fill with admiration for the unknown sculptor who could create such an incredible sculpture at the impossible most place. But why did he take such pain to create this gargantuan sculpture? Sculpting this dog must have been a unanimous verdict of the community rather than an individual's choice. The dog head has a closed and crescent right eye, mouth and a prominent and protruded nose posing as a pointer towards a hill in the distance at a bearing of 15 deg NE. There are no legends attached with it as people hardly know that the sculpture even exists here.

Dogs known as Seota or even Barwa in Mundari are acknowledged to have had very intimate relationship with tribals.

Therefore the architecture of the dog could be a memorial of a significant dog of the village or that of a significant dead person and the dog might denote his *killi* or clan.

Walking further up the hill Prantik suddenly stumbles on to an oval hole in a large boulder (Pl.18). What was it I wondered as I rushed towards his discovery? I peeped inside to find good space fit enough to be a small room.

The small shelter seemed to have been hewn out of this single large block of the stone. Whether this was the handiwork of nature or was it manmade I could not make out, but whatever be it, the place may have been used either as a refuge or as a meditating space by the wandering ascetics.

Exploring the hill I find a few more rock sculptures of a tortoise and even that of a tiger's head which could also be memorials of the deceased and the animals like the dog could represent the *killi* or the clan of the departed.

Having done with this hill we trekked to the adjacent hill but Bubu my wife and Nita, her sister decided to stay back exhausted in the hot June sun. Prantik abruptly had his right foot badly slashed by a razor-sharp stone which tore through his canvas shoes. It bled profusely; he too had to stay back.

I walked onwards, alone to suddenly encounter a superb dolmen having a capstone resting serenely on two stone posts (Pl.19). The dolmen stood pompously bracing the hot Bhandra sun which suddenly reminded me of the Devil's Den dolmen in UK; the startling similarity between these two megaliths was amazing and the monument was another evidence of contacts between UK and India in the past. I gazed at the monument marvelling at her beauty.

The hex sectioning of the dolmen was clearly displayed; it was placed at the intersection of the alignments of four hills to their respective opposites. The monument was sited between two hills on the either horizons aligned to the midsummer sunrise and the winter solstice sunset.

The area appeared to be a treasure house of various megalithic forms. A bizarre stone structure, as if it just had landed from an outer world, stood there in silent respectability (Pl.20). A tall tubular rock rose erect lifting a capstone gracefully on it crown. Was this a natural creation or was it man made, or maybe it was the handiwork of both; Mother Nature and early humans? The stone cylinder looked very unusual, there wasn't a similar looking stone nearby, but the capstone did appear to have been placed by humans at the top.

But if it was a megalith, it must have been a sacred memorial stone and in order to be so the stone was required to be in absolute alignments to hills on its either sides.

I decided to look.

Lo!

The stone stood between two hills in the horizon having azimuths of 40 degrees East of North and the dog hill at 220 West of South respectively!

A pointed part of the capstone pointed towards an unknown hill and another protrusion indicated the due east.

I could now fathom the mystery of the stone. The stone was a natural one, but as it incidentally was 'on' the alignment between two hills, the stone became consecrated for the primitives. Therefore they used it as a memorial by laying the capstone on its top and the stone was transformed into a monument.

The multiplicity of megalithic architectures fascinates me, as here was something I have never seen earlier.

2 Purni Maandar

This site was a chance discovery while roaming in the woods of Maoist infested Chatra district and crossing the timid Mohaniya River, Gyan Sagar, one of my co-workers and I hit upon this amazingly large megalithic site. What stunned me was the sheer size of the complex which spread over a length of more than a kilometre and on it we found five different sites. The megaliths of these complexes differ in their architectures indicating the temple/burials may have been built at different periods and/or may be by different tribes. The site comprises megaliths built from remote antiquity to the present times. The modern site comprises menhirs and dolmens. The dolmens which have table top capstones placed on four stone stands along with the menhirs can be seen placed in a row (Pl.21).

Little farther East, I saw a stone peeping out of dense hedges and lentils which looked like a megalith to me. I employed the local villagers to clear the lentils and shrubs of the spot and a fascinating ancient megalithic site gradually unfolded before my eyes. The peeping stone turned out to be a large trapezium shaped menhir (Pl.22). A few pillars shaped menhirs lay fallen on the ground. All the stones placed in a row have been aligned to the triangular Sultana Hill at about 210 deg West of South and the hill of Harhad at a bearing of 30 deg North East, the entire complex has been made to face the winter solstice sunrise.

One triangular tipped stone identical to the larger pointers of Rola and of the Pacahi Baba megaliths of Jabra is inclined to point towards the mid winter sunrise at about 130 degree SE. The identical pointer megaliths common in so many megalithic complexes suggest that the makers of such monuments of the region could be the same set of people. If not, then the pointer megalith was a common stone meant to transmit a specific meaning, lost with time today. I was told by the villagers that they call the large trapezoid as '*garhalwa pathaar*' or 'the buried stone'.

Walking further east I stumbled into another set of memorial menhirs of different sizes which I also found to be facing the winter solstice. Moving about 300 metres to the east there was another large burial and a memorial site teeming with hundreds of menhirs of various sizes. The largest one about 12 feet tall reclined against a lean tree flattening the part where it touched with its thrust. This stone had a row of sacred vermillion marks on it, meaning it was a sacred stone and was worshipped (Pl. 23). Like the rest of the menhirs here, this tall sacred stone too faced the winter solstice sunrise.

The villagers informed me that this is the temple of the Ganjus, a proto austroloid tribe now Hinduised, the *pahan* (priest) of this temple belongs to the Ganju tribe. The Ganjus are known for not having a megalithic tradition, therefore they may not have built the site. Various customs get mingled in a country as old and intricate as ours. I have found this tradition of megalith worshipping at many places where the worshipping community may not have erected them but they still venerate the stones as deities.

Orientation of the menhirs towards the Winter Solstice indicates the practice of *Jang Tapa* here in the past. As this megalithic site is worshipped, it is the *maandar* (a mutilation of mandir*)* or a temple. The term '*Purni*' bears the meaning of being 'old'. Purni Maandar simply translates to "Old Temple" implying to the old megalithic site which the villagers claim to be over three thousand years old. How do they assert this?

Well, sheer instinct; a valued feature of these non technological impoverished villagers, something which we modern people should revere from the bottom of our hearts.

3 BHAINPUR (PL.24)

The site originally discovered by Faiyaz Ahmed, is a chaste Mundaric *Sasandiri* burial, which doesn't seem quite old enough.

Excavation was proposed here by the State Archaeology Dept which as expected never materialised till the writing of this book. There is a dried up river adjacent to the burial evident from the channel, which was used for rituals during the funeral. The village of which the megaliths were once the burial ground ought to have been somewhere nearby.

The site is placed in the intersection of the hills in the landscape. There are over a hundred sepulchral slabs and a very few memorial *birdiri* menhirs. One near circular burial stone demonstrates good astronomy, as the vein of this rock has been used as the East West axis. However, the most enigmatic stone in the site is a solitary menhir positioned about a hundred metres South West of the burial facing the Winter Solstice sunrise.

4 BASANTPUR

I was informed of this site by one Swaminathan, a local reporter of the Hindi newspaper group "Hindustan". Once arriving at the industrial township of Ghatotand we rode on his scooter to the supposed site. Arriving there after about an hour, I realized that I was looking at a poor replica of the Punkree Burwadih megaliths.

Like PB, there were two tall menhirs, few standing ones of various shapes and many which had fallen. Two double ringed pillar menhirs were on the South Western end of the site adjacent to the tall menhirs (Pl.25). On these perhaps, once sat two amalakas of which only one was sighted in the place.

The strangest part of these two ringed menhirs was the measurements; the smaller menhir was half in height to the bigger one.

The smaller menhir displayed sides having 18" and 22" whereas the same sides of the bigger one were of 36" and 44", which means the measurements of the bigger menhir was double than that of the smaller one.

"*Amalkas*" atop menhirs signify the Hinduisation of these tribal stones. *Amalakas* on top of the two comparative sized menhirs probably denotes memorials of a King and his Queen of the region.

This is both a burial and a memorial site of the erstwhile Mundas or the Asuras which seem quite old. The *satbharwan/satgarwah* ritual of burying the bones of the deceased in small urns near megaliths or immersion of the urns in rivers is still being practised here. The rims of the urns can be seen peeping out of the sacred ground around the megaliths everywhere which is a confirmation of this ancient practice of burying the funerary urns.

One cuboid stone can be seen profusely cupmarked (Pl.26). The menhirs faced the Lugu Pahari approximately at 130 deg which is the azimuth of the winter solstice;

a feature common in this area of Jharkhand confirming the tradition of *jang tapa* of burying the stones during/around the winter solstice. To the left of the megalithic complex stood a sacred hill called Murli Tongri at 30 degree East of North.

The Lugu Pahari is sacred to many tribals. The Santals ascend the hill during Dussera under guidance of their Naike. He introduces medicinal herbs and plants found on the hill to the Santali folks and for nine days he teaches them their usage in various ailments.

To the Birhors, one of the oldest tribes of the world still living in the archaic hunter gatherer stage, the Lugu is their Marang Buru.

5 HUHUA

This is another of Faiyaz Ahmed's discovered sites near the district town of Ramgarh. The site could be Mundari by descent which does not seem to be that old but the sign of acculturation on the unique sepulchral stones is apparent. The stones here are the larger version of the ringed pillar menhirs of Basantpur (Pl.28). The site is aligned to the Lugu Pahari in the North. In other words, Huhua is to the opposite of the Basantpur megaliths which is in the other side of the sacred hill. The site is also aligned to the Sikidari hill range which is at the south of the site. Similar megaliths with *amlakas* were reported in Bajpur near Lohardagga in the late 19th century by Mr.T.F.Pepe and were subsequently recorded by Dalton[1].

The pillar menhirs have been painted in pale yellow with stripes in white and filled with a reddish brown. All the standing stones either have *amalakas* like the one of Basanatpur or have large circular female vulvar cavities on their heads. The local *pahan* or the priest who is a Munda, worship the stones during the *Maha Shiva Ratri* observed when the crescent moon of the 14th lunar day is closest to the rising sun.

The villagers inform me that they usually paint the menhirs on that day.

The villagers also revere these stones as the " *Var- Kanya*" which is a marriage cult very popular with many megaliths. This is indicative of the event that megaliths and the " *Var- Kanya* "cult is the remnant of the once prevailing fertility cult.

The ' *Var*' being the groom, the '*Kanya*' the bride and the female vaginal like holes on top of a few menhirs indicate that the ' *Var-kanya* ' cult was an accessory of the archaic fertility cult.

Many villagers believe that there is gold buried beneath the tombs.

Reference

1. Col. E.T.Dalton. Rude Stone monuments in Chutia Nagpur and other places. Journal of the Asiatic Society of Bengal. Vol, 42.

6 ASOTA

The megalith of Asota is one of the finest stone circles of the sub continent (Pl.11). Though in a ruinous state today one can easily perceive with how much grace and aplomb these magnificent stones once stood. These megaliths in Pakistan are situated near a village called Shewa.

The monument once comprised about 32 menhirs having an average height of about 3.5 meters. They are found to be placed at uneven gaps with the minimum space between the menhirs is 0.67 and the maximum is 1.34 meters. The circle had a diameter of about 17 meters.

At one time when the stone circle stood in its complete elegance two smaller stones were perhaps positioned adjacent to each other which perhaps marked the entrance within the circle.

No funerary remains have been reported from the megalith concluding which many scholars have surmised that the megalithic complex is non-sepulchral and was perhaps an astronomical observatory. This is further confirmed to the fact that the monument is still regarded as a Sun temple.

One of the menhirs has about 15/16 horizontal notches (Pl.12) which perhaps indicate to some kind of calendrical bearing corresponding to the 16 cavities of the two rowed cupules assortment.

7 LATI

This is a tiny insignificant *sasandiri* site en route Itkhori positioned to the left of the highway which one generally misses (Pl.29). The burial slabs are quite a few but the chief attraction of the megalithic site is a single gorgeous phallic menhir which has been polished to bring out the concealed yellow. This site too comprises a triangle which is made to point towards a small hill at the bearing of the Winter Solstice sunrise. The site was once the burial of a village which has long since gone living behind these fascinating stones for us to wonder at.

8 MURMA

This is one of the hundreds of the old Mundari sasandiri/janbhaga/haragarhi megalithic sites in and around Ranchi. I had initially spotted the stones from the train to Lohardagga (Pl.30).

So alighting at Ratu I walked quite a distance towards the site to find it quite near to the Jagannath Pahari in Ranchi. There is a tall stone standing adjacent to a few smaller stones placed aligned to 115 degrees which is the azimuth of the 15th Feb/26, 27th Oct sunrises. I saw a few sepulchral slabs too, on which cow dung cakes were laid in the sun by the village women to dry later to be used as high-quality fuel for cooking. Few elderly people sat guarding some playing children who informed me that this was a very ancient site existing even prior to the village was established.

Iron slags scattered all over the field perhaps indicated to the fact that the iron smelting Asurs and Karmalis were present here before they migrated elsewhere.

9 BANJHA

The name Banjha means 'infertile' which point towards the archaic fecundity cult but why such a name for a village having the female megaliths, I really do not know?

This is a large burial and memorial sasandiri/haragarhi megalithic site on the Itkhori- Katkamsari state highway (Pl.31). There are hundreds of sepulchral stones of many shapes inside the shade of this very ancient sacred grove or trees also known as the sarna. The tract is filled with Oraon tribals speaking the Dravidian Kurukh. The Oraon megaliths are a little different from the Mundaric ones. They have a dolmenoid cist with a large flat centre stone placed on four stones and a memorial menhir placed adjacent finally the monument resembling a ' kursi' or a chair, therefore is also known as 'kursidiri' (Pl.32). These cromlechs in front of the menhirs are also believed to be 'ghost seats' or even being used as resting seats for the deceased's spirit.[1]

There are not many tribals left in the area today but even the Hindus worship in the sacred grove which even they call Sarna. The main worship is conducted every alternative year during the months of *jeth* in June. The sacred stone is worshipped as "*Kudra sthaan*" or '*Badka baba*'. Badka means an 'elder' and is also a type of paddy. The worship is conducted by two iron smelting tribal Agaria Asur shamans called pahans named Jado and Mina Agaria.

The Hindus who do not understand megaliths believe the stones to have naturally evolved.

Reference

1. Col. E.T.Dalton. Rude Stone monuments in Chutia Nagpur and other places. Journal of the Asiatic Society of Bengal. Vol, 42.

10 FURUKKA

Driving right towards Punai from Ichaq More on the NH 33 one can reach the site about 15 kms from here. A lonely menhir stands alone here in the middle of nowhere. It is very silent in here but in the company of this pretty stone, you are not quite alone. You are baffled trying to figure out the reason why the stone is in here.

Is it a boundary stone, is it a memorial, is it a phallus or did it once serve an astronomical purpose for the villages here very long ago?

You are compelled to believe that the primitive megalith builders were artists as every structure they made were unique creations and not a single megalithic monument can be seen to have been repeated elsewhere. It is a pillared stone constructed with mathematical measurements. This megalith is also a major apparatus for horizon astronomy which could be established by the positioning and the hewing of the stone. The stone stands about 56 inches tall (Pl.33).

The pillar has three very sharp vertical edges of which one has been made to align towards an unknown hill in the magnetic south. The reverse edge too is very accurately oriented towards an unknown hill to its North in the remote horizon. The third perpendicular edge is made to face the true east, whether or not there exists a hill is unknown as the eastern horizon is obscured by dense trees (Pl.34).

The most exquisite part is its top part. The crown has been sloped towards the east from where one can see it has been made into a neat geometrical shape of a sector (Pl.35). Why it has been made so or how it was intended to function we have no idea. The find of iron slags also suggest the presence of iron making by the Asuras in here.

Such monuments unknown even to many archaeologists in India are sadly not taken seriously by scholars and the people alike, despite they being treasures of our nation. Such megaliths made with such astronomical and mathematical meticulousness by people unknown to us have the potentials to rewrite our nation's history.

11 BENGWA PAHARI

The region displays stunning array of megaliths; none similar to one another. This one in particular is a great dolmen (Pl.13); two capstones are seen placed on two large boulders which perform as the chamber of the shrine. The dolmen originally discovered by Faiyaz Ahmed is a few kilometres off the highway to Bokaro Steel City from Ramgarh in the Chitarpur village. Its narrative has already been enlightened in an earlier chapter. The dolmen is an engineering marvel displaying the stunning astronomical alignments.

12 MALASILI

Malasili is a village quite far from the Ramgarh-Bokaro highway where one can spot this cairn built with pieces and bits of small stones (Pl.36). The term is in actuality two words in one. Mala simply means 'garland' and Sili is 'stones'. Malasili therefore simply translates into garland of stones. Though the cairn could date back to the metal ages, it has lent its name to the village which is comparatively a newer one.

That the cairn has been made in the Recumbent Mother Goddess form surprises and this has been discussed in an early chapter.

13 PATHALGADHA

As the name suggests "Pathalgadha" means buried stones... in simple words, megaliths. The region is dotted with countless megalithic sites and each house hundreds of sepulchral stones. So dense is the spread of megalithic sites here that you fling a stone and where it drops you may bump into one site there.

The finds of many megaliths here should be credited to one Jitendra Tewary, a local correspondent of a National Hindi Daily. The megaliths here are primarily the menhir type with many of the memorial stones having placed opposite to each other in a reclining manner towards the East and West and in the process creating an extended empty row oriented towards the North and South; the position of the dead (Pl.70).

14 OBRA

Obra, originally discovered by one school teacher Binod Raj, is a ruined yet a powerful site. Most of its stones have been demolished or towed away by villagers to have them as washing stones by the well or serve as drain covers. Today only two standing and one fallen menhir is all that remains of this ancient site (Pl.38). A road running through the site has destroyed much of the ancient site. The standing stone is a beauty in itself...polished and made to stand with much dignity.

The cross in a Circle or the Hex Sectioning is demonstrated as the site stands at the intersection of the Lambayia and the Dasi hills in the North and South respectively and the Korambey hill to her East. The site is interspersed with Red, Black and also Black and Red Pottery. Iron slags lie scatter all around confirming that iron smelting tribes as the Asurs may have been present here.

That this is a Chalcolithic site is confirmed with the finds of copper objects as copper slags, a copper ring and even a small ceremonial (Pl.39) bell in a small pitcher revealed during the construction of the road.

The megaliths of Chatra are typical to the land, they are positioned on either sides giving the impression that they are about to fall as many have fallen over the passing years. But they have been planted in an incline; if one is sloped towards the east then the opposite one is leans towards the due west as discussed earlier.

15 NILURALLU

Nilurallu in Andhra Pradesh of South India is an amazingly beautiful prehistoric megalithic complex. Here it is believed that once there were more than 800 standing stones. As the name suggests in Telegu the term Nilurallu means standing stones.

However N.Kameshara Rao reports that there are about 32 standing stones and few had fallen and many have disappeared (Pl.40). The menhirs here vary from 3 meters to 4.7 meters.

One stone is profusely ornamented with 50 cupules. The site has also reported the finds of scrapers, borers and flakes. The menhirs are positioned in alignment to the equinoctial and the mid winter sunrises and sets[1]. Nilurallu therefore gives another evidence of the prevalence of complex sciences among the denizens of this lesser know civilization.

Nilurallu is perhaps one of the rarest megalithic sites in the world where the tradition of Equinox (Vernal) worship still continues in an unbroken tradition.

1. *Journal of Astronomical History and Heritage,* (2011). The Astronomical Significance of Nilurallu. N.Kameswara Rao. Priya Thakur. Yogesh Mallinathpur.

APPENDICES

Appendix 1: Relationships Between Sacred Space and Symbolism in Neolithic Britain and India

G. Terence Meaden, M.A., M. Sc., D. Phil. (Oxford)
Department of Continuing Education (Archaeology) and Kellogg College, Oxford University

Introduction

The study begins with the symbolism of the circle–whether carved, written, or painted, or whether it was designed as part of a grand monumental plan. In these respects, the circle serves as a symbol for feminine space. In India the symbol of a 'painted circle centered by a red spot speaks of masculine entry into feminine space, where it signifies an everlasting fusion of the male principle with the female principle (Fig. 1). Painted on a house wall, it becomes a well-intentioned blessing for newly-weds.

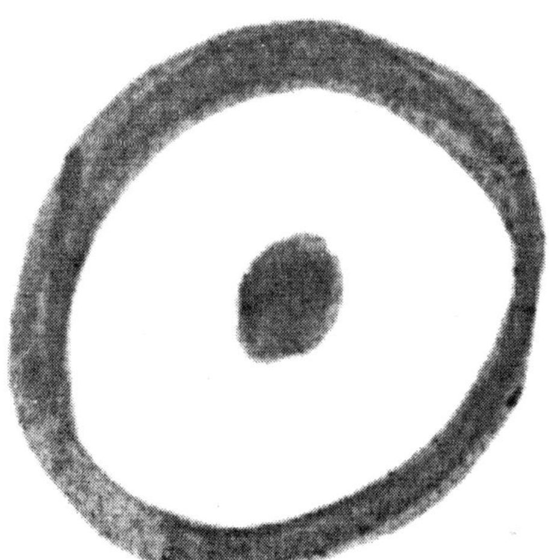

Fig. 1. Symbolic circle centred by a red spot

In Neolithic Britain and Ireland one finds the same circular artistry, either carved in stone or presented on a grand scale in the landscape of the ancients—such as a ring of female megaliths centered by a tall male stone. Of many surviving examples open for discussion, it is convenient to consider the magnificent stone circles built at Avebury in southern England between 5000 and 4400 years ago and which remained in use until about 3500 years ago.

Avebury is the biggest complex of megalithic circles and avenues in the prehistoric world. When constructed, its several hundred standing stones were steeped with symbolism—either by shape or position relative to other stones or to the direction of the rising sun, and whose interpretation is aided by philosophical and actual comparisons with what is known of present and ancient spiritual concepts in India. The discussion will help to show that in ancient times there may have been genuine contact between peoples in India and Western Europe, probably initiated by migration in pre-Indo-European times.

Avebury's Sarsen Stones

Avebury has three stone circles and two stone avenues. The perimeter of the biggest circle, 335 meters diameter with 100 megaliths, is over a kilometer. The construction is bold and massive. It centres a vast sacred landscape. Altogether, more than 600 great sarsen stones were assembled to create this 'megalopolis', with its array of megalithic and astronomical alignments. Consider the southern inner circle, diameter 105 meters (Fig. 2).

Now partly destroyed, at one time it comprised 29 megaliths around the circumference and had a single tall stone standing in the middle.

This stone, high and narrow, called the Obelisk, was the tallest stone at Avebury. It was 6.5 metres or 21 feet long, and one of Avebury's heaviest at 80 tones. Although many stones are missing because of eight centuries of destruction by Christian villagers, the positions of lost stones are known from surviving socket-holes chiseled into the subsurface chalk bedrock. What did the stones mean?

4000 years ago Avebury was in its prime. The stones are called 'sarsen stones'. They are polygonal remnants about a metre thick, caused by the cracking of sandstone beds that lay upon the chalk rock. Thus, 'sarsen' is a species of sandstone found as natural individual surface-lying rocks. In three valleys a few kilometers east and south-east of Avebury many thousands of such stones remain today, partly visible, partly buried, in the turf. 'Sarsen' is a word of ancient origin. In Wiltshire dialect the pronunciation is sassen.

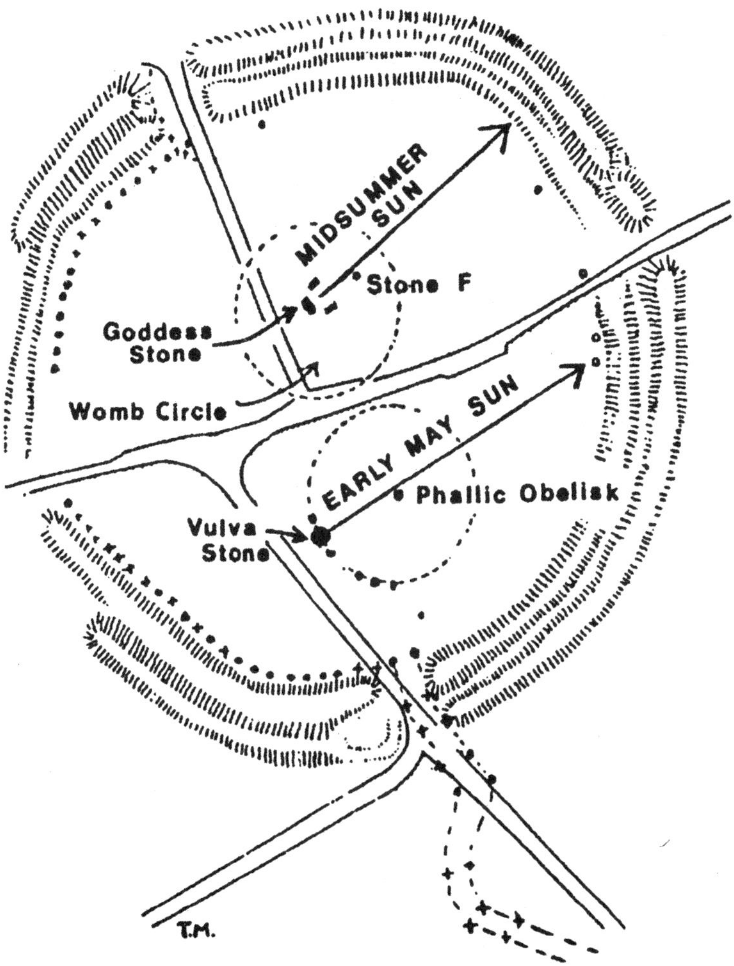

The major sunrise alignments at Avebury.

Figure 2. Sunrise features deduced for two major stones at Avebury's stone circles. Such inferences imply a ritual interest in, and links between, stones of the circles and solar movements through the year. A solar calendar for principal dates of the agricultural year is manifest by this means.

In parts of India the same archaic word–also pronounced sassen or sasan–is assigned to megaliths. Thus in Jharkhand state, eastern India, dolmens and megaliths are called Sasandiri. 'Diri' alone means 'stone'. Sasan and diri are neither Sanskrit nor Hindu.

Subhashis Das explains that the words come from an Austric language spoken by non-Hindu tribal peoples. He and I propose that the word migrated across Asia and Europe either in Pre-Indo-European times or in the earliest megalithic age.

To understand the attributes and emplacements of Avebury's stones the starting point is the proposal by Piggott and Keiller (1936) that the ancient Britons probably regarded the megaliths, depending on shape, as either male or female.

Similar reasoning applies to early cultures across Europe and Asia. Archaeologist Isobel Smith, who saw to the publication of the excavations of Keiller and Piggott (Smith 1965) articulated their collected view of the shapes of Avebury's stones with these words: "There are Type A stones which are much taller than they are wide, with sides more or less parallel and vertical, which are possibly male; whereas Type B stones are much wider, sometimes broader than their height and are possibly female. The latter are squarish, rhomboidal, or trapezium-like, while the best have the shape of a lozenge or diamond balanced on a point".

This reasoning has stood the test of time and scholarship. Indeed, it incorporates the wider view that the deities of Neolithic agricultural communities included, in ways more or less manifest, an Earth Mother and a Sky Father. We know this from written sources for numerous later societies across the historical world, and it can be inferred for many prehistoric societies too. Indeed there are nations where similar deification and devotion continue to this day (as with American Native Indians, and tribal inhabitants of India, Nepal and Borneo among others).

Authorities in symbolism deduce that all surviving perimeter stones at Avebury are 'female stones' either because of their feminine shape (as defined above) or because there are female-explicit symbols on them. It implies that each stone circle encloses female sacred space. That is to say, every circle is a womb-shrine to the Earth Mother or local goddess, as with today's Hindu temples which are womb-shaped and have a Siva-lingam icon of the male deity located in the innermost sanctuary which is the womb-cell.

The Great Seasonal Calendar that is Avebury's Southern Stone Circle

Of the 29 stones forming the perimeter of the Southern Circle five survives standing. They are female stones. At the centre was the Obelisk–since destroyed–its position marked by a short pyramidal concrete pillar. Being 6.5 metres long, if we suppose that one metre of its length was held in the bedrock, the great stone rose 5.5 metres above ground level. This tallest stone at Avebury was a male stone (Fig. 2).

For archaeological convenience the surviving members of the 29 perimeter stones are numbered 101, 102, 103, 105 and 106. In the middle of the east-facing side of Stone 106 is a fissure a metre long having obvious female characteristics (Fig. 3).

It aligns with the male Obelisk and the direction of sunrise on May Day which was 6 May in ancient times, because this day (when counting from Day 1 as 21 December) is the exact mid-point (namely, Day 137) between the equinox (Day 91) and Midsummer's Day (Day 183). May Day is traditionally the first day of summer. At Avebury the rising sun illuminates the female stone and then immediately unites male and female stones with the male stone's shadow–after which light and warmth again infuse the expectant female stone which arguably represents the Earth Mother. This is the archaic British version of the worldwide fertility rite of the Marriage of the Gods. The sunshine-and-shadow device signifies the actual mating of the Sky Father with the fertile Earth Mother.

Next is Stone 105 with its feminine circular outline. It experiences Sacred Marriage with the Sun God or Sky Father on Midsummer's Day, 21 June. In fact, the positions occupied by perimeter megaliths between south-west and north-west correspond to sunrises with respect to the Obelisk, each conforming to a specific sunrise date (between north-east and south-east) in the farming year from the December solstice to the June solstice. These directions correspond to the eight holy festival dates of the farming seasons. In summary, although some megaliths are missing, the known positions of the stones of the Southern Circle allow a complete reconstruction of the agricultural calendar that is appropriate for a British-European–and arguably Indian–Neolithic farming community.

The Northern Stone Circle

The northern circle comprised 27 perimeter stones centred by three great megaliths. Together they form a compact group called a cove, in which the broad, central, 100-tonne stone of Type B female character is flanked by a tall Type A male megalith at each side. Crucial is the recognition that the cove faces the midsummer sunrise, and that on this morning the iconic female cove stone is bathed in the light of the rising sun until the shadow of a fourth stone–a cleverly-positioned male megalith, 20 m away but since destroyed–completed the midsummer marriage by consummation a few minutes later.

It is the same at Stonehenge. Its circles represent the womb and sacred space of the Earth Mother. On midsummer morning, 21 June, the sun penetrates the great monument to its centre, and minutes later the phallic shadow of an external male

"Sun Stone" (called the Heel Stone) follows it in. Divine Marriage is consummated . It is the only time of the day, and the only week of the year, when this can happen with the Marriage of the Gods visibly achieved as viewed by the watching faithful.

It reminds us of the Kaula Temples. gives a plan and photograph of the 64-yogini temple at Ranipur-Jharial, Orissa. The circle of 64 yoginis is centred by a Siva Shrine with lingam. The monument is thought to be around 900-1300 years old. Another Kaula centre was at the Mahamaya Temple on the banks of the sacred Bhargavi river at Hirapur, 15 km from Bhubaneshwar, Orissa. It is one of only four examples of the roofless or "hypaethral" temple still standing in India. In the middle is a three-faced Siva embracing Parvati. Again, the rite of the Marriage of the Gods is being celebrated.

Concluding Remarks

The stone circles at Avebury and Stonehenge–as with other monuments in Europe–were shrines to the Earth Mother, with a cultic significance no less important than the sacred Hindu temples of India today. Moreover, from Western Europe and across Eurasia to Eastern Asia megalithic dolmens of similar type are found (Fig. 5.) The strongest evidence that dolmen builders in Europe were inspired by people who had migrated from far away in the East comes from megalithic France in which interments were accompanied by jade, nephrite and jadeite hatchets and objects of ritual character. The jade definitely originated in eastern Asia. As for nephrite and jadeite, their use, as with jade, terminated at the end of the long megalithic period, which implies either the loss of a long-distance, traditional trading source or the failure of the procurement culture. Furthermore, the Eurasian ubiquity of the cupmark carved on megaliths or rocks may share in the feminine fertility meaning of the symbolism of the circle (Meaden 1991, 1997).

Successful fertility, whether of women, animals or crops, was essential for agricultural communities. This explains the strong fourth-millennium and third-millennium interest in every facet of the annual cycle. One may envisage for Avebury and Stonehenge the actuality and opportunity for regular ritual practice, crucially involving monumental astronomy in its direct form.

The calendar was created by respecting the sun's appearance and disappearance at particular sunsets and sunrises–thus uniting monumental astronomy with festival dates and accompanying rituals. The astro-landscape solar device and philosophy are objectively practical because there is a visual symbolic or mystical linkage between sun and stone for spectators to witness. This corresponds well with the suggested thesis regarding deduced relationships between Neolithic monumental archaeology, religion, and evidence of ritual deposition (Meaden 1999).

Whatever other functional purposes may have been arranged at stone monuments, they and their surrounding landscapes were viewed as having a symbolic, mystical and ancestral significance that was at least partly interrelated with annual astronomical events. Such thinking and procedures augment a society's sense of history and affinity for the ancestral past by providing a stage for social, spiritual and ceremonial functions. By ritualising the landscape and forging an intimate relationship between people and monuments, the ancient Britons devised a memorable native tradition. Their aim, as mostly everywhere worldwide, was to improve their chances for prosperity, which they did by seeking to allay their natural concerns for fertility by calling on gods and spirits for divine aid and support. This explains the reasoning behind the visual ceremony of the Marriage of the Gods in megalithic Europe, a deep belief that persists in the Hindu recognition of the everlasting union between Siva and his consorts.

References

Keiller, A. and Piggott, S. (1936). The West Kennet Avenue: Excavations 1934-35. Antiquity, 10, 417-427 [especially 420]

Meaden, G. T. (1991). The Goddess of the Stones. 187-194. Souvenir Press, London.

Meaden, G. T. (1997). Stonehenge: The Secret of the Solstice. 48-49. Souvenir Press, London.

Meaden, G. T. (1999). Secrets of the Avebury Stones. Souvenir Press, London.

Simpson, J. Y. 1867. *Archaic Sculpturing of Cups, Circles,* etc. upon Stones and Rocks in Scotland, England & Other Countries. Edmonton and Douglas. Edinburgh.

Smith, Isobel F. (1965). Windmill Hill and Avebury. Clarendon, Oxford.

Appendix 2: The Wrap Up

For the existing humankind today this civilization of the tribals is a forgotten entity...nothing much is known of these people. In the former pages of this book I had attempted to dig into the dark obscurity of our past to find that these people had their very own language and lores, mathematics and astronomy, religion and rituals to run a civilization known very little to us.

This civilization was not quite like as that of ours... their habitats were not as enduring as those of ours nor were their creations, the megaliths which they built after profound observation and study of the transits of the sun and the moon only to desert them altogether after a time to move on to another horizon for reasons better known to them. Much, as their deities, their rituals, their understanding of the earth, the river, the wind, the horizon, their mathematics and astronomy have been usurped, loaned and taken away from them by later day emigrants into the land leaving them spurned, abused, desolate, mocked and eventually forget them to the point of shunning even the barest trace of this civilization and its denizens.

Thankfully they have left behind their megaliths all over the country as a certification of this prehistoric civilization's existence.

These fascinating primitive megaliths are the archaeological relics of this enigmatic civilization. These megaliths were their temples of their Goddesses, burials of their priests and their observatories to function as their calendars. Each megalith tells a story; a story of our predecessors' understanding of the sacred landscapes, their irrevocable reverence for the Great Goddess, their unique knowledge of astronomy and mathematics. The architecture of each megalith enlightens the beholder of the primitives' immense hunger for art and alignment, as each monument was created in relationship with the landscape which was the outer periphery of the megalithic temples.

Megaliths needs to accepted as more than just burials or memorials of the dead but as true source of this hidden civilization without which much of our hoary past will remain in befuddled anonymity.

What classical religions and modern logic failed to establish; uniformity within the humankind; megaliths succeed. Unlike the modern day churches and temples these were shrines which the primitive humankind built with near and in many places with exact similarities across the world breaking frontiers and discrepancies of many kinds.

Index

❐ ❐ ❐

PLATES

Pl.1 : Self portrait in Punkri Burwadih

Pl.2: Rural Deities carrying fish and pitcher-both symbols of fertility

Pl.3: A Santhal Manjhi Than. This temple has closed resemblance with the Canaanite Asherah altars.

Pl.4: A signboard displaying Simariya

Pl.5: A village Hindu woman donning her sindur on her head and forehead

Pl.6: A yagna in Chat

Pl.7: The Brahmanisation of the primitive Vat Savitri

Pl.8: Alignment in Birbir. Note the triangle in the foreground

Pl.9: The Stone Circle in Banadag with triangles in the middle

Pl.10: Prantik stands in the Jabra Road megaliths.
The small triangle is at the middle.

Pl.11: Asota Stone Circle. Photo credit Nawaz Ud-Din

Pl.12. The menhir in the Asota Stone Circle with the parallel notches.

Pl.13: Faiyaz sits in front of a dolemen in Bengwa Pahari

Pl.14: Cupmarks

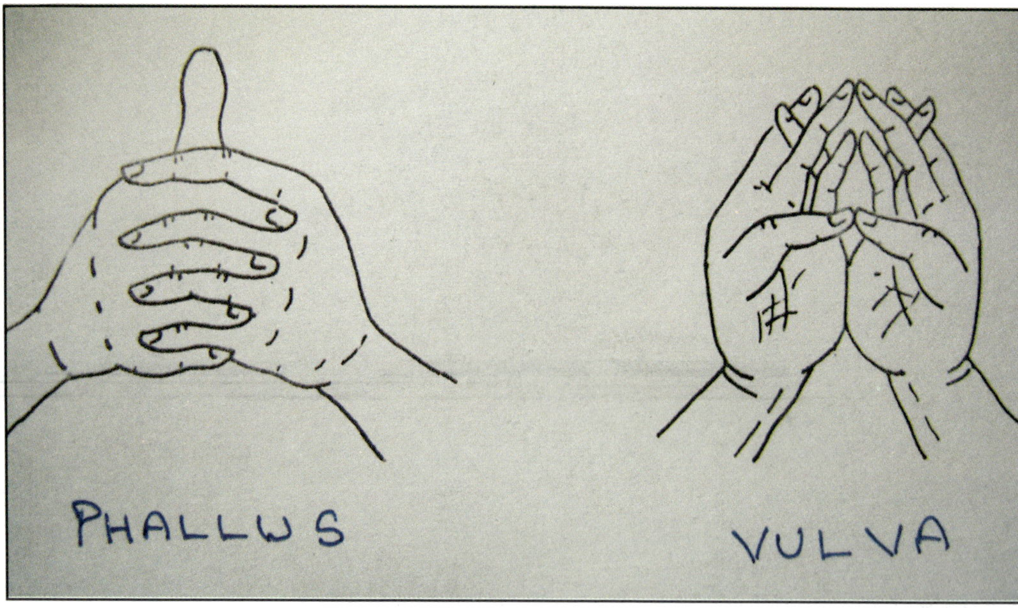

Pl.15: Finger symbols of the phallus and the vulva

Pl.16: Two rowed cupmarks in Rola

Pl.17: The dog's head in Banjha, Lohardagga

Pl.18: Prantik stands in front of a cavity on a rock in Bhandra

Pl.19: The Dolmen in Bhandra

Pl.20: The stunning natural Megalith of Bhandra

Pl.21: The contemporary Megaliths of Purni Mandar

Pl.22: Purni Mandar after cleaning (Garhalwa Pathar)

Pl.23: The Tall Stones of Purni Mandar

Pl.24: The Sasandiris of Bhaipur

Pl.25 : Basantpur

Pl.26: Cupmarks of Basantpur

Pl.27: Prantik holds the stone triangle found in the megaliths of Khunti

Pl.28: Huhua

Pl.29: Lati

Pl.30: Murma

Pl.31: The Birdiris of Banjha

Pl.32: Primitive Oraon megaliths of Banjha

Pl.33: Furukka

Pl.34: The profile of the pillar menhir of Furukka. Each edge is oriented towards Cardinal points.

Pl.35 : The frontal view of the pillar. The edges pointing towards cardinal points visible. Note the crown; it has been shaped in the form of a sector of a circle, evidence of practice of mathematics by the megalithic folks.

Pl.36: Cairn of Malasili

Pl.37: Obra

Pl.38: Obra

Pl.39 : A bell found in a small urn in a megalith in Obra

Pl.40: Megaliths of Nilurallu. Photo credit N.Kameshara Rao

Pl.41: Chokahatu

Pl.42: A dolmen in Chokahatu

Pl.43: The famous Hathia Pathhar is situated on the Damodar river and is naturally oriented towards the Winter Solstice sunrise

Pl.44: The long stone wall in Phusro emerging from the Damodar river is naturally oriented towards the Winter Solstice sunrise

Pl.45: This natural stone wall formation in the Damodar river is oriented towards the winter solstice sunrise

Pl.46: The menhir of Lohsinghna

Pl.47: Singhani megaliths

Pl.48: The female vulva shaped oil extractor

Pl.49: This vulva shaped objects are known as Gujias and are offerings of the Goddess.

Pl.50: The Mother Goddess

Pl.51: The Recumbant Mother Goddess form of the Zulzul hill with the Birbir megaliths in the foreground. The triangle points towards the Due East.

Pl.52: Malasili. See the recumbent Mother Goddess form of the monument

Pl.53: The hybrid of the tortoise and the lizard dolmen

Pl.54: The stunning framing created by the positioning of the stones in Rola

Pl.55: Rola megaliths

Pl.56: The summer solstice sunrise in Rola

Pl.57: This stone in Rola has east west orientation

Pl.58: The female dominated rural markets

Pl.59: The menhirs here have been positioned to mirror the peaks of the Tandwa hill in the horizon

Pl.60: The triangle and the obelisk have been placed in accordance to the Kesura and the Silwar hills

Pl.61: See how the tiny triangle which points to the Due East has been positioned here to replicate the Kesura Hill in the background

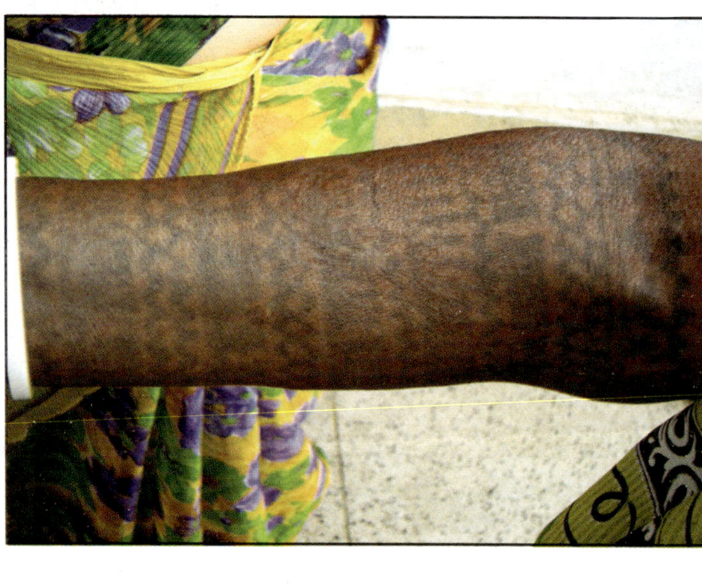

Pl.62: The zigzag patterns of the tattoo are similar to the zigzags of the rock arts in Isko

Pl.63: Primitive rock art in Isko comprisng the zigzags

Pl.64: This Malasili pond could have been been
a circular henge prior to its conversion into a pond

Pl.65: These inscribed lines having a east-west orientation were
possibly used as a calendar. Chalk is smeared for visibility

Pl.66: The sunrise of 20 Feb and 26 Oct in Punkree Burwadih

Pl.67: The sunrises exactly between these two menhirs on the equinox mornings in Punkree Barwadih

Pl.68: The equinox sunrise in Vibhuthihalli

Pl.69: Two menhirs in Punkri Burwadih frame the Recumbant Mother Goddess form of the Amjhori Hill

Pl.70.The menhirs are positined to the opposite inclined towards the East and the West